Praise for the Dating Goddess

The Adventures in Delicious Dating After 40 series of books is based on the blog Adventures in Delicious Dating After 40 at www.DatingGoddess.com. Here are comments from readers.

💜 "Adventures in Delicious Dating After 40 is a wonderful composite of both the mechanics of post-40 online dating and what the practice of honoring one's self actually looks like. How marvelous your writing is to read. I spent about 2 hours reading and was riveted the whole time." —Maggie Hanna

💜 "At last, a dating writer who addresses requirements. You are SO right on! I'm thrilled to have found you!" —Rachel Sarah, author, *Single Mom Seeking*

💜 "Powerfully heartfelt and honest writing. You are inspiring." —Kare Anderson, Emmy Award winning writer

"I just love your writing. It is very fresh and gives the reader something to think about." —Kelly Lantz, President & Manager, 55-Alive.com

"Dating Goddess, you are like a, a, a, well, a goddess to me. You've helped guide me successfully through my re-entry into the dating world after 14 years. I'm an eager student and fast study, and do get myself into situations that others don't know how to deal with — such as 3 dates in one day -— so thankfully you are there! You're the greatest, thanks for all you do for us!" —Jae G.

"I find your point of view much more interesting than other dating writers. Thanks for always reminding me to enjoy dating life no matter what it throws at you." —Sandy

"I love Adventures in Delicious Dating After 40. I really do like your honest and authentic voice — it's refreshing." —Wendy S.

"Adventures in Delicious Dating After 40 is really fun to read. Thanks for sharing your thoughts and letting us divorced single women know that we are not alone. There's a lot here that I identify with, although I'm not as brave as you are about dating lots of guys. So far. Love your blog — the first blog I've ever read consistently." —Elizabeth

"Thanks for a wonderful blog. You're doing a great job of saying what's in my mind. There's rarely a day I miss when it comes to checking in on your wisdom." —Paulette Ensign

Real Deal
or Faux
Beau

*Should You Keep
Seeing Him?*

by **Dating
Goddess**

Real Deal or Faux Beau: Should You Keep Seeing Him?

Second Edition

Cover design by Dave Innis, www.innisanimation.com

Book design by JustYourType.biz

Printed in the United States of America.

ISBN   Print: 978-1-930039-40-7

         eBook: 978-1-930039-19-3

How to order:

The *Adventures in Delicious Daing After 40* books may be ordered directly from www.DatingGoddess.com.

Quantity discounts are also available. Visit us online for updates and additional articles.

The Adventures in Delicious Dating After 40 books are dedicated to my ex-husband since he unexpectedly released me to explore the untethered life of a single woman. I then had the freedom for the experiences, lessons and insights shared in these pages.

Books by Dating Goddess

💜 *Date or Wait: Are You Ready for Mr. Great?*

💜 *Assessing Your Assets: Why You're A Great Catch*

💜 *In Search of King Charming: Who Do I Want to Share My Throne?*

💜 *Embracing Midlife Men: Insights Into Curious Behaviors*

💜 *Dipping Your Toe in the Dating Pool: Dive In Without Belly Flopping*

💜 *Winning at the Online Dating Game: Stack the Deck in Your Favor*

💜 *Check Him Out Before Going Out: Avoiding Dud Dates*

💜 *First-Rate First Dates: Increasing the Chances of a Second Date*

💜 *Real Deal or Faux Beau: Should You Keep Seeing Him?*

💜 *Multidating Responsibly: Play the Field Without Being A Player*

💜 *Moving On Gracefully: Break Up Without Heartache*

💜 *From Fear to Frolic: Get Naked Without Getting Embarrassed*

💜 *Ironing Out Dating Wrinkles: Work Through Challenges Without Getting Steamed*

Contents

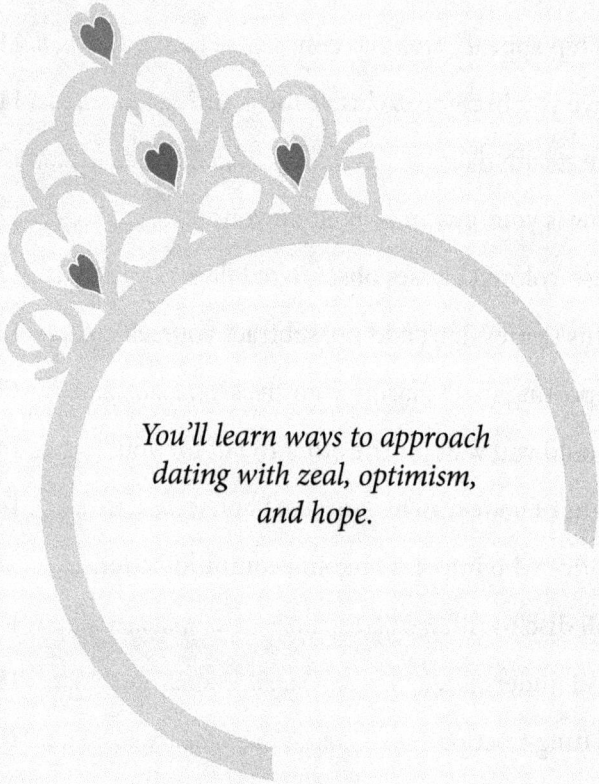

You'll learn ways to approach dating with zeal, optimism, and hope.

Introduction

This book is designed for anyone who is interested in stories, advice, and lessons from the midlife dating front. If you are over 40 and haven't dated in a while — or even if you have — you'll learn ways to approach dating with zeal, optimism, and hope. Even if you've had more than your share of negative experiences, I'll share how to glean lessons from those adventures, rather than just declaring that "all men are jerks" or "men are just looking for sex."

While most of the perspective is from a woman to women, men's comments, experiences, and lessons have been integrated as appropriate.

This book began as daily entries into my blog, Adventures in Delicious Dating After 40, which has been featured in the *Wall Street Journal* as well as on radio and TV. I wrote about my epiphanies from my and my friends' dating life. The best postings were culled to make this and subsequent books.

This book focuses on second dates and beyond. During the dating process you are both assessing if you want to keep seeing each other. This book helps you see what questions you need to ask yourself.

xi

This book consists of three types of perspectives:

Lessons: These are specific experiences I thought would be useful to you. A few lines from my experience illustrate the points.

Insights: These usually start with an experience I've encountered, then the insights that experience spawned. It is usually comprised of around half story and half insight.

Stories: These are examples of situations I've experienced — or was currently experiencing when I wrote that piece — that I thought would be entertaining. Or I thought the story would help you see what kind of things happen in the midlife dating world so you'd know what has happened to others.

Because these writings were real time, as they occured, they are often set in the present tense. But they are not chronological. So a reference to "my current beau" may now be many sweethearts ago. I hope this isn't confusing.

I'd love ot hear your stories and questions. Please email them to me at Goddess@DatingGoddess.com. They may make it into the blog or my next book!

Who is the Dating Goddess?

I am a middle-aged, white, professional woman. My husband of nearly 20 years left me in April 2003 when I was 47, 11 days shy of 48. After giving my heart time to heal from the surprise divorce sprung by the man I thought was my soulmate, I started dating 18 months later. Generally, I have had a great time meeting interesting men, some of whom became romantic beaus, some became treasured friends, and some I never heard from again.

> I am not a well-preserved, gorgeous, marathon-running middle-aged women

In the beginning, I had dates with single male colleagues, but I quickly found Internet dating was the way to explore the most "inventory" and qualify men who I thought might be a good match.

I am not one of those well-preserved, gorgeous,

marathon-running middle-aged women. I have been told I am attractive, but I am overweight and not a gym rat. So while I am active, I do not match the description 90% of men's profiles say they want: slender, athletic, toned, fit. I have some wrinkles — what one sweet suitor mistakenly called dimples. I have what Bridget Jones called "wobbly bits," as most non-surgically enhanced middle-aged women do. My genes — and a lifetime addiction to chocolate — have made their mark. Yet I've met and dated some wonderful men, so even if you're not a lingerie model, you can find guys who will think you're attractive, perhaps even hot!

In my professional life, I am a bestselling author of workplace effectiveness books, professional speaker and management consultant. I've appeared on Oprah, 60 Minutes, and National Public Radio and in the *Wall Street Journal* and *USA Today*.

This book is intended to not only be useful to others and cathartic for me, but is also the genesis of a new topic for fun, thought-provoking speeches. I'm calling myself a dating philosopher and giving date-a-vational speeches! Let me know if you know a group who would like an entertaining after-lunch speech on how lessons learned from dating have implications in business and personal relationships and well as life philosophies.

How did I come by the Dating Goddess moniker? After a few months of dating dozens of men — one week yielded 7 dates with 6 guys in 5 days — my friends dubbed me this name. I liked it, so it stuck.

I'm purposefully not sharing my picture as I don't want you to think either, "How did she get any dates at all?" or the opposite, "Of course she found it easy to get 112 men to ask her out." I am not hideous (usually) nor am I stunning (without professional hair, makeup and Photoshop!). Some men find me attractive, some don't.

I continue to search for my "one," but I have learned a lot along the way, and my single and not-single friends have loudly encouraged me to share my experiences and lessons in the hopes of helping others navigate the adventure of dating with more success. And to have a delicious time doing it!

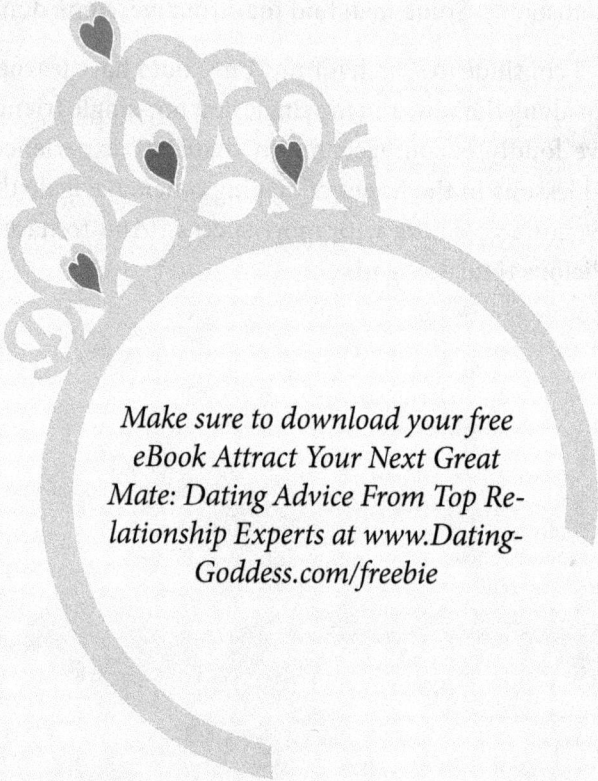

Make sure to download your free eBook Attract Your Next Great Mate: Dating Advice From Top Relationship Experts at www.Dating-Goddess.com/freebie

Care of newbie daters

Many midlife daters reenter the dating scene after a long absence. If they aren't a longtime single, they are available again because of divorce or death of their partner. At this age, many are sensitive to fading looks and possibly squishy bodies, even though others are more buff and more attractive than ever before. Midlifers are more aware of their shortcomings, which can overshadow their pride of accomplishments, both career and personal. And they aren't sure exactly what is expected of them during the dating process. They are a bit fragile at first.

If you've been dating for a while, especially if most of your dates have come from online sites, you've learned some of the ropes. You are more savvy now than you were as a neophyte dater.

If you are an experienced dater, I think you have some responsibility — even if it is just for your own karma — to treat newbie daters with kid gloves. Not that you wouldn't do that with everyone, but I think it's especially important to help guide new daters through the process, sharing with them what you've learned during your dating experiences.

For example, I learned from an experienced online dating gal pal that it is expected for you to exchange emails after the first date to express if you want to see the other again or not. I would not have known this was considered a common courtesy if she hadn't enlightened me. I would have assumed I would hear from the man if he was interested in seeing me again. So I made it a habit to always email the guy within 24 hours of our first encounter to thank him and express whether I was interested in doing it again or not. Many times he initiated that email or even called after the date.

Because of your experience, you know that many online daters see multiple people simultaneously, so you can't assume the guy is seeing only you. If you are starting to see a fledgling dater, explain that it is common to go out with multiple people, each once or twice before deciding whether to focus on only one or keep looking. So be upfront if you are dating others. And even if you're not seeing others, you might drop this information into the conversation so they know to ask a future date outright.

You also know that it is unfortunately prevalent for people to stop responding to calls, emails and IMs when they don't want to continue dating someone. So even though you are careful to clearly communicate you're not interested in a man any longer, help him understand this regrettably common practice so he won't be scratching his head when it happens to him. So if you decide to stop seeing this dating novice, take extra care to communicate you're moving on as graciously and gently — yet clearly — as you can.

I've found that those who haven't dated much or in a long time can easily become attached to you if you are just your usual nice self. I think it is because they have not had much (any?) attention or affection in a long while. If they get a single, attractive woman to look them in the eye, smile and carry on a fun conversation for more than a few minutes, they think they've found The One.

I once had a coffee date with a man who had just filed for divorce after a 25-year marriage. I was his first post-marriage date. He was giddy during our coffee, talking about plans for taking me here and doing that together. I knew I was not interested in seeing him again, so I encouraged him to take advantage of his new-found freedom and date a number of women to really find out what he wanted and who was a match. So even if you only see him once, you can be a mini-coach to him, sharing any hard-won wisdom you've gleaned so he's not blindsided with what you know are common midlife dating behaviors.

I had a second encounter with a widower who lost his wife of 30 years the previous year. I may have been his first dating experience in over 30 years. So I was conscious of making sure I treated him with tenderness and care.

What advice would you share with a midlife dating tenderfoot? What have you learned the hard way that is more common than you'd imagined before you started this adventure?

Deciding to see him again or not

Even when there isn't the immediate physical attraction or chemistry, I'll sometimes see a guy again to see if there is any underlying spark that needs a second chance to be kindled. If there was nothing abhorrent on the first date, I may try once more.

If there was nothing abhorrent on the first date, I may try once more

For good example, a gentleman arrived on time and wore nice, pressed casual clothes for our second-date stroll to my local neighborhood dance party. He didn't try to maul me with kisses and too-soon affection — in fact we only hugged hello and goodbye.

However, during the stroll and dinner, he interrupted me a lot — something that is a pet peeve of mine. While he did seem interested in what I was saying, he also often tried to summarize what I said — but he was wrong each time. I am usually a clear speaker ,and when others summarize they most often get it right. So it was clear he and I weren't thinking along the same paths, and it got annoying after a while to keep correcting him.

So the bottom line question for me is, "Do I want to spend more time with this guy?" Do I find him interesting — or appealing — enough to invest another hour? While I'm easy going and can find interest in nearly anything, if there isn't enough to keep me interested, it's best to let him go. I'm afraid that is my conclusion about this man.

Are you in agreement that you're dating each other?

I recently read that a man can go out with a woman 2-5 times (or more) before he considers them dating. A woman often leaps to that conclusion on the second date. (A male friend even suggested that some of us consider we're "dating" a guy we haven't met yet, only talked to by email or phone!)

There are some circumstances where it could be nebulous. Perhaps you are workmates, gym mates, or classmates and you invite each other for coffee, a hike, a movie, or over to your house for dinner. Maybe you either go Dutch or take turns treating. Or one picks up the movie and the other dinner. Even if you are physical, like cuddling during a movie, unless there's some smooching, it still can be nebulous. And sometimes even making out isn't a sign that you're dating.

In "What is the definition of a date?" (in the *Date or Wait: Are You Ready for Mr. Great?* book) I shared my early confusion about what constitutes a date.

After dating a man a handful of times, with plenty of smooching, I made some reference to "our relationship." He adamantly corrected me that we weren't in a "relationship." I asked what he called what we were in then. He said we were "hanging out," and "seeing each other." I don't know when "seeing each other" becomes "a relationship" — at least in that guy's mind. I'm guessing it has to do with deciding to be exclusive. Interestingly, we "saw each other" for 6 weeks before he told me in an IM that we shouldn't see each other again. I guess that if we were "in a relationship" I might have earned a breakup email instead.

> *I don't know when "seeing each other" becomes "a relationship"*

Some people have told me that meeting for coffee with someone from a dating site isn't a date. It's a "meet" to see if you want to have a date. I could argue both sides. Fundamentally, to me a date is when you spend time with someone to explore if there is romantic potential.

Because of this ambiguity, I'm told that some men don't get into "date" mode until the second, third or more encounter. Because he hasn't decided to woo you, he sees no need to call regularly, dress nicely, or show other signs that he's interested in you. He's in "I like her, but not sure I'm that interested in her" mode. So if you think "second dates and beyond mean we're dating and he needs to woo me with calls, flowers, etc.," you're setting yourself up for frustration. If you get on his case about not calling, he'll be out of there in a flash if he doesn't realize you're in different places. If he sees he needs to step up his romance or lose you, he will if he's interested. Otherwise, he may have the "let's be friends" talk.

At what point do you consider yourself "dating" a guy?

Avoiding a trip to Abilene in dating

I have nothing against Abilene. I've been to Abilene, KS, and it was a nice town, home to the Eisenhower Museum. I've not been to Abilene, TX. But I'm really talking about the metaphor described in the management education film called "The Abilene Paradox."

In the film, adult family members are visiting their parents and discussing what to do on this hot, humid afternoon. A few possibilities are floated. Someone suggests going to Abilene for dinner. Another agrees, and pretty quickly they are packing themselves sardine-style into the old, air-conditionless car and making the hour-long drive. When they return four hours later, they sit on the porch trying to cool off and recuperate. Someone finally says that the trip was a debacle, and another says she only went because she thought the others wanted to go. Soon everyone has chimed in that they didn't want to go, but only joined because they didn't want to be a spoilsport.

Now, back to dating. Have you ever done something like this? You and the guy you've dated six times are discussing what to do on a summer Saturday. He says, "I'm open. What would you suggest?"

Here's your moment of truth. You'd really like to sit on the shady back patio and read your book alongside your guy while sipping lemonade. However, you think he'll think that's boring, and by implication you are boring for suggesting it. You're still in that wanting-to-impress stage.

You've heard him talk about how he used to take his kids to the beach, so you suggest something you think he'll like. "I know — we could go to the beach." You hear yourself saying this even though you don't like the hassle of beach parking, you burn quickly so have to douse every exposed skin cell with sun screen, and you aren't fond of just sitting in the hot sun. The water is too cold to swim, so spending hours floating isn't an option. However, "Are you crazy?" never crosses your mind because you want to propose something you think will please him.

He says, "Sure" agreeably but not enthusiastically. Soon you are sitting on the beach in your long sleeves and hat, with every exposed part slathered in SPF 1,480,272 sun block. You feign enjoying yourself so you won't appear wet blanket-like. After several hours, you return home and are both relaxing on the patio with lemonade. You say, "This is the life. It's so lovely right here. I wish we'd just stayed and relaxed here all afternoon."

"What?" he exclaims. "I would have loved that. The

beach was okay, but I don't go very often because of the crowds and the sun, and the water is too cold to swim. I used to take the kids because they loved it, but it was never top of my list of great places. I only went because I thought you wanted to go."

You just went to Abilene — no matter where you really went.

Even though I've known the Abilene paradox story for 20 years, I still find myself going there occasionally, just as you might. While I've gotten much better at telling the truth about what I want and don't want, I still get detoured down the Abilene bypass once in a great while. It happened recently.

> *I've gotten much better at telling the truth about what I want and don't want*

A group of 10 gal pals convened in San Diego. We made reservations for the Hotel del Coronado for dinner. For various reasons, only five of us attended. It was a beautiful restaurant, right on the water. However, instead of asking for a table outside, we dutifully followed the hostess to a windowless private dining room set for 10. While this would have been fine for a large group, it was too big for the five of us. None of us thought to ask to be seated outside. But if we had, we would have not only enjoyed the evening air and the ocean's waves, but could have basked in the private fireworks show for the wedding reception held at the hotel. We heard the pops, but saw nothing.

Even among this group of highly successful, asser-tive businesswomen, none of us seemed to want to rock the boat and bring up moving. Only afterward did we discuss how dumb it was to be cooped up inside. If we hadn't gone to Abilene we would have had a once-in-a-lifetime experience.

Have you gone to Abilene with dates? How have you learned to avoid this trip to nowhere?

Talk is cheap

W hile I believe that words are very important, actions are equally important. So if a guy tells you how much he's attracted to you or wants to be with you, but doesn't take actions to see you he is just stringing you along. If he gives you excuse after excuse, just let him go. He'll tie up your heart and energy, when he isn't really serious about seeing you.

I once dated a man for six months who lived an hour's drive away. He called me every day at least once. He'd promise to come see me the next day, yet something would frequently "come up." He would actually fulfill his promise only every two to three weeks. I put up with it for a while; however, I let him know I was disappointed. I finally got tired of having a no-boyfriend boyfriend, so I told him I wanted a break. I wasn't willing to put up with his daily lack of integrity.

So, if he says that he's a gentleman and he cares about you, yet treats you disrespectfully, his actions and words don't match. You deserve someone who has the integrity to act congruently with his words.

What's your date's Delight/Disappointment Scale score?

Competitive people keep score. They note accumulated points and penalties. I think we do this with our dates, but it's usually unconscious.

I've devised a chart to illustrate what usually happens in our minds. We track the things we like and weigh them against the things we don't like or are disappointed by. Sometimes these disappointments are things that are said or done (watching TV over your shoulder when out to dinner, insulting something dear to you — even if unwittingly). More often disappointments are things not done (didn't call when he said he would, forgot promises or important dates).

"Tracking your date's score" (in the *First-Rate First Dates: Increasing the Chances of a Second Date* book) suggests a guy starts with 100 units or points. He can earn more by doing things you like and loses points for disappointing you. I know this sounds harsh. But the truth is we're doing this mentally anyway, whether or not we actually assign points to the actions/inactions.

Look at the following chart to see how I think we track these points on the Delight/Disappointment Scale. Notice this guy's score hovers around the mid-point — he doesn't do a lot to delight nor disappoint. Then New Year's Eve came with no invitation. (One of my pals said, "This guy doesn't get you and how to treat you!" I'm afraid when I look at the chart, I'd have to agree.)

Maybe you don't want to be as analytical as keeping a chart like this. But I do think it is important to be conscious of how he comes out on the Delight/Disappointment Scale. We can all handle disappointments when someone is on the positive side of the scale most of the time. No one is perfect, and we are bound to disappoint the other at some time. However, if there are too many trips to the south side of neutral it's time to reassess the relationship and discuss it with him if you have been dating for a while (he deserves to know so he can fix it if he wants), or move on.

How does your current guy rate on the Delight/Disappointment Scale?

Your Date's Delight/Disappointment Scale

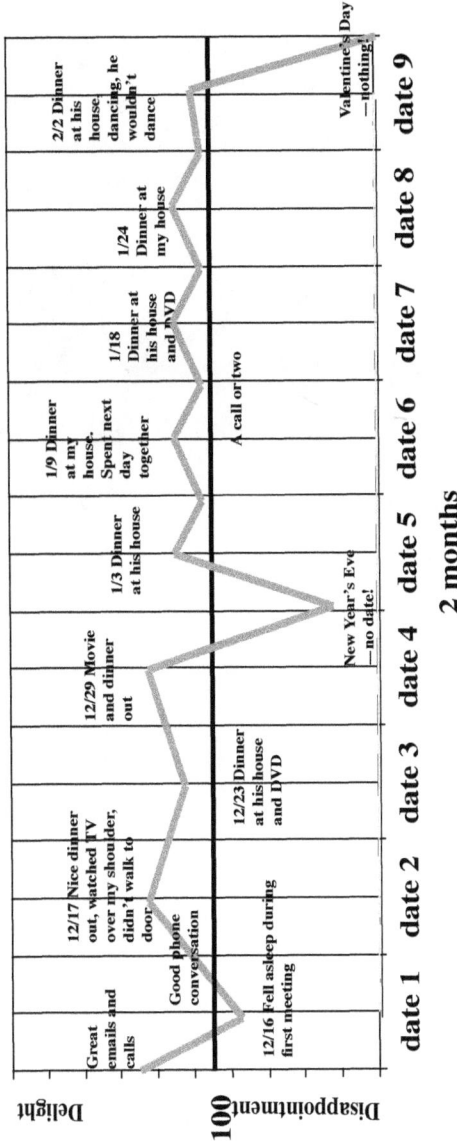

Delight

100

Disappointment

date 1	date 2	date 3	date 4	date 5	date 6	date 7	date 8	date 9

2 months

Great emails and calls

Good phone conversation

12/16 Fell asleep during first meeting

12/17 Nice dinner out, watched TV over my shoulder, didn't walk to door

12/23 Dinner at his house and DVD

12/29 Movie and dinner out

New Year's Eve —no date!

1/3 Dinner at his house

1/9 Dinner at my house. Spent next day together

A call or two

1/18 Dinner at his house and DVD

1/24 Dinner at my house

2/2 Dinner at his house dancing, he wouldn't dance

Valentine's Day —nothing!

19

The date relationship test

I've discovered a key relationship test. This one is guaranteed to tell you what you need to know about your guy, so I recommend using this test early on to decide if you want to keep seeing him or not.

What is the test?

Picking a DVD together at Blockbuster.

Why is this such a good test?

You will see if he only wants to see gory, action flicks and if he has any tolerance whatsoever for romantic comedy or chick flicks. I know, I know, I'm stereotyping. But you get my point — you see how comparable your tastes in movies are, and more. Maybe you like indy films

This will tell you what you need to know about your guy

and he only likes sophomoric pics. Is he open to seeing a movie you like, even though he doesn't regularly watch that type? And if he insists on seeing "Saw" even though you tell him you hate scary movies, he's not listening to you.

How do you negotiate? What if you have a difficult time finding something you both want to see? This process will tell you a lot — a whole lot — about the guy you're going out with. I've learned this process tells you quite a bit about your guy.

A guy pal tells me that when a man agrees to watch a chick flick, he's really just hoping he'll get lucky after the flick is over. Are we surprised?

Build a relationship bridge one stand at a time

When you begin to date someone you like, your shared experiences connect you together. You're building a relationship bridge.

Each experience creates small strands of the bridge's supporting cables. The laughs, smiles, gentle touches, kisses, phone calls, emails, and kindnesses are spun into stronger cord. As time goes on, the cord is twisted into rope, then cable. The more threads of positive experience, the stronger the eventual cable which helps keep the relationship bridge suspended.

However, when there are disappointments, harsh words, or forgotten promises, the threads become frayed. The strain begins to unravel those caringly created cords. They can be repaired, but only with consciousness and thoughtfulness. If left in disrepair, other strands will break, and the bridge will be lost.

I ponder why a guy would ignore me for a month (or several) then call and expect to pick up where we left off. I wonder if he has any idea how my connection to him hangs by a thread — or perhaps has been severed entirely. Or how tenuous the strand is with the guy who calls regularly but makes little effort to see me. Yes, he's adding strings by calling, but not nearly as quickly or strongly as when we see each other.

What are relationship-building threads for you? What are the little things that add to the bridge or break it down?

"*Let it please be him*"

In college I remember singing Vikki Carr's "It Must Be Him" whenever a lovesick roommate would be awaiting a call from her new beau and the phone rang. Vikki's pleading "Let it please be him, oh dear God" is how I feel now when I'm awaiting a new suitor's call. He didn't say when he'd call, just that he'd call. And I long to talk to him. I haven't heard from him in three days.

"So why don't you call him?" you ask.

If I call again, will I appear desperate?

"I left him a message yesterday. I don't even know if he's back from his business trip. Maybe he's still gone. If I call again, will I appear desperate? Everything I've read says the man should long for you. He should pursue the woman. If she sounds too available and needy, it's a turn off."

You wisely counsel, "Cell phones work in all parts of the country. Even if he were busy, he could find five

minutes before he went to bed to call you. If he were flying yesterday or today, there's plenty of waiting time at the airport for a quick 'Hello.' No, you shouldn't call again."

And so I busy myself with other activities so as to not focus on the phone not ringing. I hate this part of dating.

"What size bed do you prefer?"

This is a favorite question to ask a guy I've been flirting with for a bit. Depending on the chemistry, it is not a first-conversation question, and perhaps not even a first-date question. But if he is fun and flirty, then I'll ask.

It tells me a lot about him.

Whatever he answers I ask, "Why?" That gives me the info I want to know. It's a piece of the puzzle.

If he says, "King," I ask why. He then may say, "I like my space. If I'm going to have to sleep with someone, I don't want to keep running into her all night."

All righty then. I know this guy is not into midnight contact, let alone cuddling. I'm into snoozing and snuggling, so this would leave me feeling out in the cold.

However, if he said he liked a king bed because it gave us more options for activities and we could spread out the Sunday paper as we curled up in each other's arms, I'd know we were on the same track.

One guy told me he was claustrophobic, so sharing a less-than-a-king bed meant he couldn't sleep. I'm a touchy-feely person, so this did not bode well.

Another man answered, "Queen." When asked why, he said, "I like to be near the woman I'm sleeping with. I like to put my arm around her waist, spoon and pull her close." Yep, right answer. Go to the head of the class. My kind of guy. (Of course, there are other criteria, but this was a good start.)

How would you answer the question and why?

Broaching tough conversations

In talking with a married gal pal, we discussed how sometimes it is hard to bring up difficult issues to your mate. I shared that there were things in my marriage that I wish I'd brought up, but instead kept them to myself. She agreed that she was withholding some difficult topics in her relationship as well.

However, in dating there is a freedom to bring up challenging topics. Often the reason you wouldn't bring something up is because the risks are too great — you're afraid of losing him or damaging the relationship irreparably. But when you're dating, there is less risk, as if he responds poorly to the topic being brought to the table, he's not a good match for you if you like to discuss things openly.

In dating there is a freedom to bring up challenging topics

So not to bring something up out of fear is not do-ing either of you a favor. You withhold something you'd really like to discuss, and he misses the opportunity to explore it with you and find out what's on your mind. If he responds angrily (assuming you aren't blaming him or accusing him), he's not able to discuss difficult issues rationally and maturely. Wouldn't you rather know that early in the relationship rather than after you've invest-ed months in this guy? I would.

"*I want to respect me in the morning*"

Y ou know the old ploy of a guy wanting you to sleep with him. He says,

"I'll respect you in the morning."

But what about you? Will *you* respect you in the morning if you allow yourself to be seduced?

A man I'd dated a few times tried to get me to allow him to stay overnight, promising we'd "just cuddle." While part of me was tempted, I knew how I'd felt in the past when I'd given in to such requests, as cuddling, even clothed, can easily lead beyond.

Will you respect you in the morning

So I had the presence of mind to respond, "I'm sure you'd respect me in the morning. But *I* want to respect

me then, too. So we're not going to spend the night together tonight."

He couldn't cajole his way around that, so we went our separate ways that night. And it was true — I did respect myself more for stating my boundary and sticking to it.

What do you need to respect yourself in the morning? Be clear on your limits so when you are tempted to waffle, you hold the line. Think about how *you* want to feel about you — not how you want *him* to feel about you — and your choices will be much easier to make.

Trust your instincts

Have you ever found yourself in a situation because you didn't follow your instincts? Your gut is saying, "Danger, Will Robinson" but you ignore the flashing red lights.

I never thought I'd have to remind myself of this sage old advice: "If something doesn't feel right, get out of the situation — now." I am a confident, assertive, strong woman. I am clear (or so I think) on what I want and don't want. Yet, in 3.5 years of dating, I've been surprised how this image of myself has been tested. I've ignored my instincts and sometimes allowed myself to be enticed into things I wouldn't have thought I'd do.

Once in a great while I've been with a man who, when I've said "no," will say something like "Five more minutes," "Then let's just kiss/cuddle," or "C'mon, I'll behave." Then he proceeds as if I'd said nothing. Now I've learned not to give in to pleas, no matter how good what we're doing feels. It can lead to doing what you don't want to do.

Saying "no" is hard for many women, as we are typically socialized to be agreeable, sometimes to our detriment. Even strong women can be seduced by smooth talking and cajoling. If we like the guy, we don't want to send him packing. But if he doesn't listen to and heed what you want, he's not for you, so he should be sent on his way. If he doesn't honor your boundaries, how would he ever respect your desires in other parts of your potential life together?

If he doesn't listen to and heed what you want, he's not for you

You might say, "At some level, you want to be doing what you're doing unless he is physically forcing you. As long as you can stop it and you don't, you must want to keep going."

You might also say, "You are sending mixed messages by saying 'no' then giving in to his requests. No wonder he doesn't believe your 'no.'" Mixed messages are never good.

So now I watch what happens when I say "no." If he honors it, I know he respects me. If he doesn't, he's putting his own needs ahead of mine. That's not a match. So if he doesn't respond to your "no" the first time, get yourself out of the situation — and the relationship.

Does he invite you to his place?

A friend called:

"I have a new lesson about dating." She's been dating longer than I so I was interested in what new wisdom she'd gleaned.

"Spill," I coaxed.

"Before you get too involved with someone, make sure you go to his home. If he doesn't have you over, he may have another woman in the picture." Sigh. It is true.

I dated a man for six months who refused to invite me to his house. His excuse was plausible, although strange. He was living is a very small mother-in-law quarters while his house was being remodeled. It was used for storage so had just a path between boxes and stacked furniture to get to his bed the bathroom and the kitchen. While I protested that I didn't care, he was adamant that he didn't want me to see it because it was such a mess. Hmm. And perhaps because of another women's clothing in the closet?

There were no other indications of another woman, so I tolerated this situation until it — and other strange behaviors — made me call it quits.

My friend's lesson came from insight of a male friend of hers. For the last month she'd been dating a wonderful man, someone about whom she was excited and with whom she could see a future. A week ago they were supposed to get together at his house, but he called and cancelled the date using a flimsy excuse. That was the last time she heard from him, when previously he had called every day. When lamenting to her male pal, he explained how some men operate. Luckily, I think it is very few men, but there are those who are into the game.

It is a good lesson. If he doesn't invite you to his house within the fifth or sixth date (assuming you've invited him to yours), something is up. It may not be another woman, but an obsessive "privateness" or no interest in taking the relationship deeper. I dated one man for six weeks who never invited me over. I never found out why, but I can guess.

Instead of roses, he gives you ... lingerie

On our fourth date he announced, "I bought you a present."

"Oh?" I inquired, "What?"

"I'll give it to you later."

At the end of the evening he handed me a bag. It was a silky negligee.

This man had never even given me flowers, but he gave me lingerie! My husband of 20 years never gave me lingerie, but this guy does on the fourth date. The good news is he got the size right, something my ex never could figure out even though he had easy access to my closet and drawers.

Most women agree lingerie gifts are for the man, not the woman. He likes seeing you in sexy things, so he buys them "for you." He doesn't know that they chafe and pull and are uncomfortable. He likes how they look on you. Luckily, most of them don't stay on long.

I have been given some interesting presents from my beaus. Some of them were appropriate. Others were more for him than me, like the lingerie.

An early beau gave me a set of "right"-sized red wine glasses because he didn't like the shape of my crystal ones. Since I don't drink red wine, this set of 12 was for him (and picky guests I suppose) when he drank red wine at my house. He also gave me a Blackberry which didn't sync with my Mac. He wanted me to have it so he could intercom me anytime he wanted to reach me. Calling wasn't sufficient? While I appreciated the thought, I asked him to take it back since it would cost me $100 a month in charges for something I didn't want and wouldn't work with my computer.

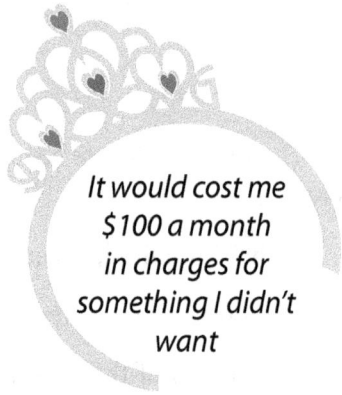

It would cost me $100 a month in charges for something I didn't want

However, some beaus have given me presents I was grateful for at the time and still am. They weren't necessarily the romantic gifts that are appreciated most, although I am fond of the two semi-precious-stoned rings one boyfriend funded. The gift that reminds me of him every day is a new faucet head he bought and installed to replace a broken one that dripped incessantly.

Other simple but appreciated gifts include a new kitchen timer when my BOM (boyfriend of the month) learned my old one broke. One former suitor passed on a nice living room chair and a glass coffee table that match my decor perfectly. When he got new furniture for his new post-divorce house, he offered them to me. I'm glad I was the recipient of his good will — and the pieces.

Sometimes the gifts are of labor and expertise, rather than tangible. One guy affixed a stereo antennae so now I get more radio stations. Another greased my garage door opener, lubricated my locks, fixed a broken towel rack, and waxed my car. Yet another unclogged a downspout. And one sweetheart helped me fix a jammed CD player.

Presents, from the wrong person, can have emotional costs affiliated with them. The garage-door-opener greaser/lock lubricator/car waxer did so without checking to see if I wanted these things done. I thanked him and thought I showed my appreciation, but not as much as he thought I should. So I said, "Thank you for doing these things for me. I know it is part of how you show you care for me. And I'd be even more grateful if you'd help me with things I've identified need to be done." He got huffy and said I was taking advantage of him. He wasn't around long.

Giving someone what they want instead of what you want to give them seems to be a hard concept for some men to grasp.

And sometimes gifts aren't, really. In week five of a six-week relationship, a man who works on Macs for a living offered to give me a part I needed. When he brought it to me, I offered to pay for it, even though it sounded like he was going to give it to me since he had it laying around his office. He accepted my offer, and said, "Cash, please." I was incredulous. "Really? You're kidding." He said, "No, I'm not." He wouldn't take a check from a woman he'd been dating regularly for over a month. No wonder we stopped seeing each other shortly after that. Maybe he knew a breakup was imminent so thought I'd put a stop payment on the check.

Not surprisingly, the same gift from different guys can evoke wildly different emotions. I've received three teddy bears from different guys during my dating adventure. One was on the first date from someone who has become a dear friend after we decided we weren't good together romantically. I think of him fondly every time I see it. The second was a much larger bear from the Mac-repair guy mentioned above. At the first opportunity I sold it in a garage sale as I didn't want anything around to remind me of him. And the third was a first-date gift from a man I instantly fell for — unrelated to the bear.

The best gifts, I've learned, are those of the spirit. Kindness and thoughtfulness trump any tangible gift. But material gifts selected with some thought are meaningful as well. For example, I always appreciate flowers, but when a man learns I prefer unusual flowers, like bi-colored roses, peonies, anthurium or protea, I feel even more cared about. It shows he's taken the time to learn my preferences and acts accordingly. But no matter what the gift, I always appreciate at least the thought and effort behind it.

Paris & Rio — right invitations, wrong guys

I've been invited to Paris by two guys. In fact, one guy asked me twice, 15 months apart, and I wasn't even dating him the second time. And I never dated the other guy.

I did not accept the invitations.

Why?

The first time, with the twice-asker, I had just been dating him a few weeks. On the third date, in early December, he said, "Would you like to spend New Year's in Paris?" Duh! Of course! However, at that late date there were no flights that would get us there and back in time for an unchangeable commitment I had.

The second invitation came from a colleague who has flirted with me — and I back — for years. He was going to Paris next month, and would I like to join him? While the invitation was enticing to accompany someone who visited Paris often so would know where to go and what to see, I'm not fond enough of him to pal around with him for days on end. He can have a grating personality that can get old fast. Although I'd insist on separate rooms, he can be forceful and I didn't want to spend a week fending him off.

The third invitation came when I spent the evening with my old beau at a bar with some of his friends. They were organizing a cruise through Europe with a week in Paris. He asked "Do you want to come with me?" While I'd love to go, I knew that to go as friends would be problematic. He'd want to spend the days together — and would probably try to spend at least one night. While I like him in short spurts, he is hard to take in long spells. And he'd insist on paying for dinners, etc., even if I tried to pay for my own. Then I'm afraid I'd feel obligated to spend more time with him than I'd enjoy.

I knew that to go as friends would be problematic

One friend said, "Why not just go and enjoy it? He even offered to pay!"

Because if I did, I'd be sending mixed signals, one that I just want to be friends, and secondly that if I accept his generosity, he'll expect certain boyfriend privileges. I'm not willing to do that. That is akin to being a prostitute in my mind.

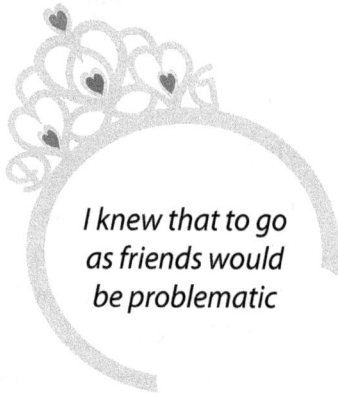

Then in one week, two other men asked me to accompany them to Rio! One invitation came before I'd
even met the man! The other was from a man I'd dated
twice, but then heard from infrequently. He also asked
me to accompany him on a week-long cruise. But I
hadn't spent enough time with him to know if I'd feel
trapped bunking with a man who may have unshown
character flaws. And I felt he was really just seeking a
presumed guaranteed week-long booty call.

So the bottom line is: no Paris, Rio or cruise with
these guys. But I like that the invitations were offered,
so when I've found Mr. Right and he asks, I'll say yes for
the right reasons. Don't sell out your principles just for
an exotic trip.

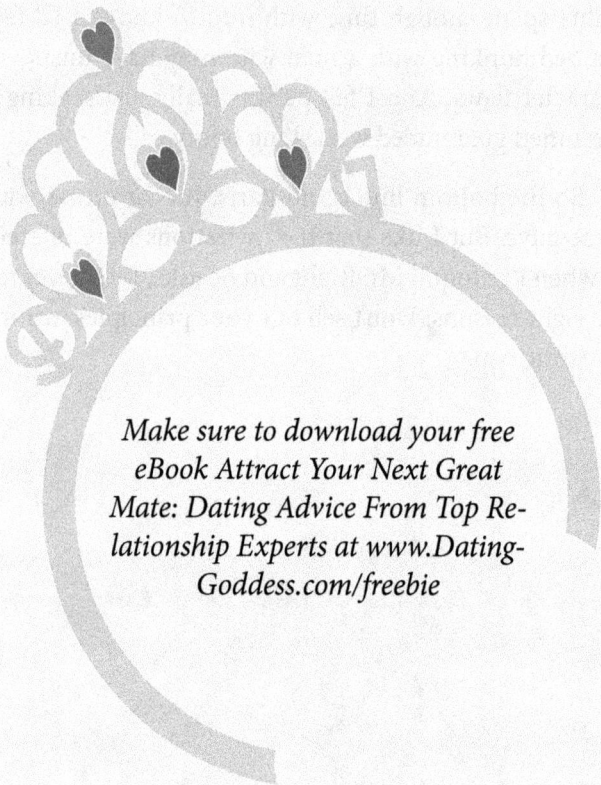

Make sure to download your free eBook Attract Your Next Great Mate: Dating Advice From Top Relationship Experts at www.Dating-Goddess.com/freebie

"What's your ring size?"

You'd think that this would be high on the list of a single woman's most-desired questions to receive. Unfortunately, for me it was not.

We'd been dating for four months, although we saw each other only every 10-12 days. He called every day, but we hadn't really spent much

I didn't feel enough emotional closeness to feel bonded

time together. I was fond of him, but didn't feel enough emotional closeness to feel bonded. So when he asked my ring size on the phone, I was surprised.

"Why do you want to know my ring size?" I asked curiously.

"Because I want to buy you a ring."

"Why do you want to buy me a ring?" I asked gently, hoping he wasn't going to say it was a promise or engagement ring.

"Because I want you to have a bauble to wear and think of me." I silently exhaled since he didn't go where I thought he was going.

After sharing my ring size, he asked what kind of ring I would like. As I began describing the size, color, and stone I wanted, he said, "Go to hsn.com." We shopped virtually and I showed him the ring styles I liked.

I thought he would order one and present it to me. Within hours, I received an online gift certificate for the Home Shopping Network. While the thought was sweet, the execution was less than romantic.

I was able to buy two rings — one garnet and one amethyst— with the certificate. And even though we broke up a few months later I do think of him when I wear them. But I don't think it had quite the effect he was hoping for!

Him or someone better

Do you know the prayer, "This or something better"? It is commonly used when you are awaiting some good news — a new job, new client, offer on a new home, college acceptance.

Sometimes I've wished that it will work out with a new guy and he will be "The One." He seems great in so many ways. But we're just starting to date, so I don't know how it might turn out.

I'm tempted to wish he is "The One." If I hang onto that desire too strongly, I become nearly obsessed waiting for his calls, imagining our life together, planning the wedding, etc. — after only a few dates.

So to get past this yearning, I've started practicing an adaptation of the prayer. My version is "Let him be The One, or someone better." So if he is not the one (which is how it's worked out so far), there is plenty of room for "someone better" (as in a better fit for me) to come along.

Try it the next time you seem besotted with someone in the early stages of the relationship.

Boomerang boyfriends

I got a call from a guy I had one date with four months ago. He wanted to see if I was available.

I've had guys break up with me and a week later want to get back together. I call these boomerang boyfriends. You stop seeing each other for whatever reason. Perhaps you both date other people, and then they contact you again. After dating others they think you two had a good thing. Or they don't date and get lonely, so they get back in touch.

After dating others they think you two had a good thing

With only two exceptions, I've found it is too late to try to reignite interest. I've moved on, started seeing other people. One exception was with a guy who kept in touch while I was seeing someone else, and when that relationship ended, he was right there. Another was with a man who beguiled me but then went poof for five weeks. We had lunch to decide if we wanted to try again. We did, and it lasted another five weeks before it fell apart.

Do boomerang boyfriends work out? Who's to say? If you were sad that the relationship ended, maybe give it another chance. But if you're clear there is a fatal flaw that would prevent you from wanting to be with that person long term, see if you can move to being friends. Some don't want that, but some do. Just be clear what you want and don't take back someone who isn't a good fit just because you are lonely. It won't work.

He's baaaaack!

This phrase may conjure up images of Arnold Schwarzenegger in "The Terminator 2." The man I'm referring to has a few of Arnold's characteristics — an easy smile, intelligence, humor, confidence — and nice biceps!

In "Boomerang boyfriends" I discussed guys who get back in touch after months without contact. My hunch is they get lonely and liked my company, so they want to see if we can rekindle what we had before. Or they are horny and want to see if they can get a booty call. Which they can't.

I got an email from a guy I went out with two times several months ago. We had a good time (or so I thought) and seemed to enjoy each other's company. Then poof — he was gone. He went on a weeklong business trip and said he'd call, but didn't. I emailed him once and called once, but I got no response — until today.

His email said he's been abroad for a few months. They don't have email abroad? I know they do where he went. He said he was busy taking care of his sick mother. While that sounds noble, I'm sure if he thought I was important he would have found time to zap me a quick email once in a while.

He asked if I was seeing someone steadily. When I said no, he asked if he could take me to dinner that night.

He had some alluring qualities but some rough edges as well. He's 12 years younger than me, so he has some not-quite-as-mature-as-I'd-like behaviors (although I've learned this really has nothing to do with a man's age!). I decided it was worth an hour or so to catch up with him, so I accepted the dinner invitation.

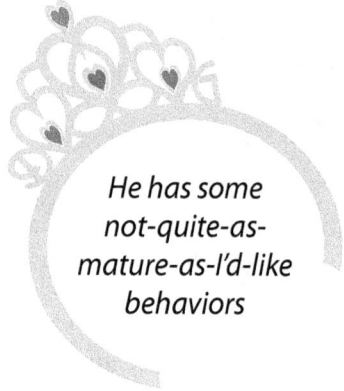

He has some not-quite-as-mature-as-I'd-like behaviors

At dinner, he asked why I didn't have a boyfriend. We like to banter, so this playful dialog ensued.

> *"There are several vying for the boyfriend position, but no one has secured it yet."*
>
> *"I want to apply."*
>
> *"Let me tell you some of the requirements and see if you're still interested. My boyfriend has to call every day, even when traveling domestically. If you're abroad, an email will do, although we could also do Skype."*
>
> *"I'll call you every day."*

"Good. While I don't mind occasional spontaneous outings like tonight, you need to ask me out several days in advance."

"I'll make sure to make an appointment a few days in advance. In fact, I'll do it now for Friday. Do you want to go dancing?"

"Let me check my social calendar. Yes, that will be fine."

"Good. We can decide the details when I call you tomorrow."

"Good. You have to do better at chivalry — opening doors, etc."

"I do open doors!"

"No, you don't."

"My last girlfriend didn't like that, so I stopped. I'll work harder."

We laughed and teased as I reeled off other requirements. I was reminded why I had liked spending time with him. He was fun and could laugh at himself and made me laugh. And he was cute, smart, generous and affectionate.

So while I think we both know he won't get the long-term boyfriend job, we will have fun hanging out together. And while my "requirements" may seem demanding to some, I think they're pretty basic for any dating relationship. If he wasn't willing or interested in some of these requirements, he could say, "I'm really just looking for someone to go out with periodically" and that would be fine.

Wouldn't it be great if both people would be this up front with every potential relationship about what is really needed to make it work? Typically on a first date or call, the question is asked, "What are you looking for?" And the responses aren't too revealing. "I want someone to love me for who I am and I want to love them for who they are." Sounds enlightened, but it is trite.

I think most of us are looking for the combination of over-arching philosophical agreement (values, goals, beliefs) with the day-to-day behaviors that, for us, mean love. Thus the calling and chivalry for me are everyday actions that show me he cares enough to please me.

If you haven't begun your boyfriend job description, you can get some ideas from "What's your 'perfect boyfriend's' job description?" (in the *In Search of King Charming: Who Do I Want to Share My Throne?* book).

You can tell a lot by your date's ... driving

I don't recommend you get in a date's car until you've gone out with him at least three or four times. But when you do, notice how he drives. It will tell you a lot about his personality. Here's my take on driving habits and what they can tell you.

- *Tailgates* — He's impatient and somewhat reckless. If you say something and he gets defensive, he's not open to feedback and doesn't care about your comfort and sense of safety.

- *Swears, complains* — If he frequently swears at other drivers or continually complains about traffic, he doesn't know how to let it go. There's nothing he can do about traffic, so why complain?

- *Weaves in and out of traffic; cuts in a too-tight space* — Impatient, trying to jockey for position. This dangerous habit will gain 1-2 minutes. Who cares—— unless you're going into labor in the car or bleeding all over it!

♥ ***Doesn't use turn signals*** — He doesn't care that his actions have impact on others, so he sees no need to communicate what he's intending. This may be a portent of his lack of communication with you.

♥ ***Goes exactly the speed limit in the fast lane*** — Even though others are passing him on the right, he insists on staying in the fast lane because "I'm going the speed limit. They can go around." Can we spell "control"? He justifies this obnoxious behavior because he is "right" and ignores that he is a traffic hazard.

♥ ***Passes people who are in line on exits and on ramps, then squeezes in*** — No regard for others. Thinks his time is more valuable than others. Takes glee in saying, "What suckers!" as he passes them on the shoulder. This man has problems.

♥ ***Gives others the finger*** — Lack of anger control, not willing to give others any grace. If he gets angry over something so trivial, what will he get angry at you about?

♥ ***Speeds excessively*** — Lack of regard for laws, recklessness, trying to show his bravado. He isn't showing his respect for your safety.

♥ ***Goes through yellow signals at the last minute*** — Most accidents on city streets happen in intersections. People jump the green and hit those who are in the intersection when it turns red. His disregard for the yellow warning is reckless and self-focused on his desire to not wait the 90-120 seconds for the next green light.

Stomps on the gas at green lights — He thinks driving hard shows how manly he is. I think it shows how stupid he is, as he'll waste more gas, burn through more tires, and possibly get in a wreck with those who, like him, are impatient so blow through yellow lights.

Rolls through stop signs — He uses the excuse that "There's no one around" to ignore basic traffic laws. This shows he does not understand the concept that character is what you do when no one is around to see.

Multitasks — if he tries to drink coffee, eat, talk on the cell phone and change the radio station/CD all at once, he isn't paying attention to his driving. He will probably multitask with you, as well, not giving you focused time.

Honks — there is little need to honk unless there is an immediate danger. Honking to express anger is immature.

Shows consideration of others — If he lets in those trying to merge and generally is considerate of others, he'll probably show consideration for you as well.

Drives safely — He's showing he respects his, yours and others' lives. He is conscientious and alert. He may display those characteristics in his relationship with you.

If he is riding in your car, you can tell a lot about him, too.

💟 ***He tells you where to turn, even though you're familiar with the area*** — If he doesn't ask if you'd like his assistance, this is the sign of a control freak. If you say something, his response will be, "I'm just trying to help." He doesn't realize that you don't want his help unless you ask.

💟 ***He tells you where to park*** — He is treating you like a child who can't see a parking place on your own. There is a difference, however, between "Park there" and "There's an empty one over there." One is a demand and the other is a suggestion. If you want his help finding a space, ask.

💟 ***He unjustifiably finds fault with your driving*** — "You're such an old-lady driver," "Just pass this idiot," or "Can't you go faster?" Tell him to shut his trap unless there's a danger or you ask for his opinion or help.

What else have you learned about your date by driving with him?

The "Better Than Nothing" guy

In my friend Susan Page's bestselling book, *If I'm So Wonderful, Why Am I Still Single?: Ten Strategies That Will Change Your Love Life Forever* she discusses the "Better Than Nothing" (BTN) partner. A BTN is someone you know isn't "The One," yet you hang onto him because you feel it's better to have someone than no one.

> *You hang onto him because you feel it's better to have someone than no one*

I've been in a BTN relationship. And I think he felt similarly. He lived a few hundred miles away, and although he called every day, he only made one trip to see me in 6 months. I visited him twice combined with business trips to his city. He still called daily, so I know he had some interest in continuing the connection. It felt like we were in a BTN relationship.

Why stay in BTN relationships? You know you have someone who will accompany you to a wedding or party, if needed. You can probably count on him for New Year's Eve. It gives you some security, like the spare tire in your trunk, even if you don't use it much. Just like the tire, you know it is temporary.

If you are exclusive with your BTN, you deprive each other of finding someone who is a much better fit. If you aren't exclusive, your BTN is the "spare" you have to fall back on if others don't work out.

How do you know if you are the other's BTN? By the lack of motivation he shows in seeing you or calling you — in other words courting you. If he's lackadaisical about wooing you, you are, no doubt, a BTN.

Do you tell him that he isn't "the one" but you'd still like to see him? In other words, that he's a BTN? If it seems he's more serious about you than you are him, then yes, let him know. It is only fair. I would avoid using the BTN wording, but let him know you don't feel he is "the one." Then he can choose to continue seeing you, or not, but at least you're honest.

What do you think of BTNs? Have you been in a BTN relationship? Why did you decide to continue or break up?

Coupon use on a date: savvy or cheap?

This may seem like a silly issue, but it came up.

A gal pal shared that she was a bit put off on a first date by a guy pulling out a 2-for-1 coupon when the bill arrived. Even though he was paying, she thought it made him seem chintzy.

On the one hand, it showed he knew how to stretch his dollar. And since he was paying, why not get the biggest bang for his buck? On the other hand, it made it seem like the only reason she was along was so he could use his coupon. It didn't make her feel special.

She asked for my input. I suggested that if he approached it differently he might have seemed less like a skinflint. When he tendered his invitation, he might have said, "I'd love to take you to lunch to a new restaurant I've been wanting to try. And I'm hoping it won't offend you, but they've even given me a coupon to dine there. Will you accompany me?"

By setting it up this way, he's telling her in advance

and making it sound like a special place that he's heard of and wants to try.

In fact, on two occasions when a new guy and I have been discussing where to meet, I've thrown in the option of a place where I have a coupon. "I have a $10 off coupon at Left at Albuquerque, if you wouldn't be embarrassed that we use it." Then he can decide if he wants to go there or not.

Another time as the bill came, I said, "If it wouldn't bother you, I have a $15 coupon." My date was very happy, not embarrassed.

When time for the check, if you decide to split it, the coupon amount comes off the top and you split the balance. Don't say, "Well, the coupon covers my share." Tacky!

Does he mention you to his pals?

Most over-40 women have close pals with whom they frequently share their dating stories and woes. If she is at all interested in him, her gal pals know about a man soon after contact is made, even if just through an email. After a date, she may share the details with more than one close friend, or even her mother.

However, my midlife male dating pals tell me it is less common for them to share with their buddies that they are dating someone, and if they do, it takes longer for the information to come out than for women.

In fact, it's common for a man to be uncomfortable when he hears the woman he's seeing has talked about him to her friends or relatives. In some way it feels a bit constricting. He prefers that whatever they do and talk about is just between them. He doesn't like that others know what they discussed or are psychoanalyzing his behaviors.

A woman is thrilled when she learns the man she's

been seeing has told his friends about her. She feels that means he really likes her — just as Sally Field exclaimed those many years ago. "You like me. You really, really like me!" His sharing about you implies he has long-term intentions. And when he tells his mother about you — wow! That's a big step.

Your ego is pumped up when you know you are being "bragged on" to others. It shows some sense of desired longevity in the relationship when others in your "tribe" are in on the adventure. A past beau didn't even tell his best friend about me, even though we dated for two months.

I realize some people are more secretive than others, and they are concerned that talking about a parade of people makes them seem like losers. Obviously, that's not an issue for me!

Where are you on this issue? Do you tell your friends immediately upon receiving an interesting potential suitor's contact? Or do you wait a while to share? Do you tell him you've shared about him, and if so, after how long dating?

And when you hear he's mentioned you — either directly from him, or when you meet his friends and they say, "We've heard about you" how do you feel? What if you've been dating regularly for a few months and the relationship seems to be progressing, and you learn he hasn't mentioned you to his best friend? How do you feel then?

Are you stingy in dating?

Stingy: unwilling to give or spend; ungenerous.

When most of us hear the word "stingy" we think of miserly, penny-pinching, Scroogelike, tightfisted, cheap and skinflint.

You could be one of these things in dating if you never offer to pick up a tab, buy tickets, or buy even a nominal gift for your guy. Male friends complain bitterly about women they've dated for months who never offer to buy an ice cream cone, cup of coffee, or movie popcorn. Even if he makes many times the money she does, guys still appreciate it if the woman makes some effort to share the economics of dating.

> *You could be singy if you never pick up a tab*

However, when I speak of "stingy" I'm thinking more along the lines of the second part of the definition

— ungenerous. This includes withholding compliments or nice comments about things you admire or appreciate in your date. It can be as simple as, "You look good," "You smell nice," or "I appreciate your taking me to dinner." A man I dated for two months did not utter one compliment to me other than before we met — and that was in an email. While I feel I took every opportunity to compliment or acknowledge him, there was a dearth of this coming back to me.

Some folks are stingy when it comes to sharing important thoughts or feelings about themselves, as they are then vulnerable. I once took a personal growth seminar that encouraged us to share with others what we'd learned about ourselves in the session. Through this sharing we provided an opportunity for the listener to relate to our epiphanies, get to know us at a deeper level, and perhaps see they could experience similar breakthroughs. We were told the more we shared with others, the more generous of spirit we were. And our insights might be the inspiration the other needed to do some work on their own lives.

In dating, at least at first, we don't let our dates hear our innermost thoughts and fears. Generally, it is good at first to keep the conversation at a more surface level, as we need to trust our date won't think we're wacky or needy, and we don't want to hit him on the head with our overstuffed baggage. But if you don't share yourselves as you get to know each other, the relationship is based on superficial conversation — the weather, sports, celebrities, food, etc. When you begin to share yourself

— your goals, fears, dreams, hopes, hurts, feelings — is when you begin to be generous with your soul. That is when true connection happens.

Sometimes this generous sharing happens early on, and emotional bonding takes place quickly. You may have had the experience I've had where because of the depth of our sharing, I felt I'd known the person a long time even though we are only first meeting. I love sharing at the soul level, but I've also then fallen too hard too fast with someone who wasn't really a good match.

What do you think about stinginess in any of these three areas? Have you felt yourself being less generous than you know you could be?

The dangers of idealization

On a third date, a guy and I shared how well we got along and how well matched we seemed to be. He surprised me when he said, "Don't idealize me." I hadn't been. I was clear on his imperfections, yet I was enjoying the parts that I liked.

It can be easy to idealize someone after a few dates if he seems to fit your perfect-guy criteria. "Falling in lust" (in the *Ironing Out Dating Wrinkles: Work Through Challenges Without Getting Steamed* book) described a different man: "There were no red flags — is that a red flag that he has no immediately detectable flaws?"

Seeing no detectable flaws is a sign that you are idealizing. Another is when you feel yourself falling head over your Jimmy Choos within the first few dates. You are overlooking potential red — or at least yellow — flags.

You may say, "What's the problem with idealizing? Isn't that what being in love is? You only see the positives of the subject of your ardor?"

Idealizing means you barely notice any foibles. And if you do observe them, you dismiss their being a problem. He's always late for your dates? He just gets distracted at work. He didn't remember your birthday? He has so much on his mind he forgot. He doesn't apologize when he inconveniences you? He means to, but it's hard for him. And on and on we go, offering excuses to anyone who asks.

However, what if he idealizes you? One man I dated came close to this. It seemed I could do no wrong. And if I did something like be late for a date, although I called to let him know I was stuck in traffic, he brushed over any hint that I could do anything untoward. While it was nice to have the ground beneath my feet worshipped, I knew it also meant that I would be tumbling from my pedestal at some point. That time came seven weeks into our dating when he emailed me that he'd like us to just be friends. I don't know how long chunks had been falling from my marble column.

So while it can be exhilarating to be in the bliss of adoring someone so much you hardly note the gnats of his failings, it is also dangerous, as it's easy to lose your heart, and with it your common sense. Best to have the strength to ask a few good friends what they see, and not get defensive when they point out what your blind spot is blocking.

And while it can be flattering and ego enhancing to be on the receiving end of idealized adoration, know that it is not healthy. Your eventual fall from the pedestal can be painful if you don't help your devotee see that his effusiveness is not entirely warranted.

"What's in your wallet?"

While this has become an advertising slogan for a credit card company, I hope you don't say it to a man you're dating. Just as most women protectively guard the contents of their purses from inquisitive eyes, men protect the contents of their wallets.

So imagine my surprise when a CEO I was coaching asked me to help him go through his wallet and pare down the contents. He was embarrassed by its bulk protruding from his back pocket, and he refused to carry a man bag. While I thought this was more a job for his wife, I agreed since he was paying me handsomely. It was interesting to get up close and personal with the contents of a wallet belonging to someone other than my husband or a beau.

On several occasions, when a man I was dating invited me to go through his wallet, I figured he must have nothing to hide, so I dug in. In some cases, I've discovered items secreted away in crannies that he'd forgotten were there.

The discoveries always gave me a broader picture of the man.

One man's wallet held not only the requisite drivers license, credit cards, cash and picture of his daughter, but membership cards to some clubs I didn't know about. But most telling were the two — count them two — condoms he had stashed. Some single men commonly carry one, but I thought two was interesting. Did he want an extra in case one broke? In case his spontaneous fling begged a reprise? He didn't say.

Another guy's wallet didn't house a single picture of his son. Most men carry at least one picture of their kids, even if the photos are ancient, but this one did not. Weeks later, in his home I noticed that there were no pictures of family, either. Not his son, sister, brother, parents, etc. Not even in his bedroom. It turned out he was not much into family — or people, actually — and wasn't close to any of them.

He didn't have a single picture of his son

And one man's wallet was particularly interesting to me. I playfully quizzed him about various components, including his Screen Actors Guild card, even though I knew he wasn't an actor. We talked for 30 minutes on sundry items and I got to know him better in the process.

So if a man invites you to explore his wallet, and you're comfortable doing so and want to know him better, take him up on it. The experience is like a treasure hunt — you'll discover gems that will help you get to know other parts of his life.

Just know he may want to root through your purse or wallet in return!

Warning: Don't ever go through his wallet without his permission, as it's an invasion of privacy. You wouldn't want him doing that to your purse or wallet.

The money talk

A 63-year-old gal pal has been dating her 70-year-old boyfriend a few years. They recently returned from a fabulous vacation. I asked her how they worked out expense sharing.

She said since he makes significantly more than she does, he pays for hotel, dinners, and other large expenses. She buys breakfasts and simple lunches. She may pay her air fare, but when they are first discussing the trip, if she doesn't feel she can afford it, she tells him. If it's something he really wants to do and wants her company, he'll pay all or part of her airfare, too.

I asked how this evolved. She said that they talked about it in the beginning and have just worked it out as each case came up. Her beau is not a wealthy man, but he is working and has wildly variable income. When he's flush, he's very generous. When he isn't, they don't do as many luxurious things.

They live in different cities. He comes to see her more often than she to him. She cooks nearly all meals when he's at her place, so they figure that evens things out a bit. They may go out once or twice when he visits, and he generally picks up the tab.

It interests me to understand how dating couples work out financial details especially after dating for a few months. When my ex and I dated, neither of us had much money. We'd take turns buying dinner and a movie. And we didn't do anything that was costly. After we were married, we generally split everything 50/50, although if I was having a good year and he wasn't, I'd subsidize our vacations. This never happened in reverse.

When I've gone out with affluent men, I've not made a big deal out of taking turns buying dinners. I tended to buy the movie if he bought dinner, or I invited him to my house for dinner. "Are you stingy in dating?" (page 65) shared that even well-off men like it when a woman offers to buy him coffee or an ice cream cone once in a while. And if a man had an income similar to mine, I'd tell him I'd like to take turns buying dinner or lunch so it was more balanced.

"Go dutch or accept your date's offer to treat?" (in the *First-Rate First Dates: Increasing the Chances of a Second Date* book) discussed some people's tendency to insist on going dutch when dating. The effect is not always a positive one. The same is true when nothing has been said about your treating ahead of time and the check comes. Your date picks it up and you snatch it out of his hand. It often leaves him feeling emasculated.

How have you worked this out when you've dated someone longer than a few months? Have you discussed it explicitly, or let it happen in the moment?

The working date

I was interviewed by a *Wall Street Journal* reporter on the concept of working dates. Does this mean you bring your date to work, as you would bring a son or daughter on those "bring your kid to work" days? Does it mean you agree to have a date where you do chores around the other's home?

No, neither of these. It means you have some work that must get done on the weekend or in the evening, yet you also want to see your sugar. Does it work to have a working date? It depends on how you work it.

I've had a number of working dates, all with guys I've been seeing for a while. So let me share some guidelines:

- *Only suggest a working date when you have built up trust with the guy.* It can be off-putting if you suggest a working date as the second date, as it implies he's not interesting enough to get your full attention.

- *Agree that it will be a working date before you get together.* Don't spring it on him as he (or you) arrives, "Oh, by the way, I need to spend a few hours on my presentation for tomorrow. I hope you don't mind." Some men will be flexible and watch TV or read a book, but some will resent, it as they expected to have your focus.

💜 *Invite him to bring some work or reading after you explain your need to get some things done.* It's cozy to sit on the couch with your sweetie reading together with some body parts touching. This can even work if you both have a laptop.

💜 *Accept that a working date may not be what he wants.* If you tell him before you get together, he then has an option to do something else for the evening. Don't take it personally.

💜 *Set some ground rules.* For example, don't check your Blackberry every 10 minutes unless you've told him you're expecting an urgent email from a client or your boss. If you are at an event or restaurant, if you need to respond, it is best to excuse yourself to the restroom to take care of business.

💜 *Agree on an end time.* If the deal is take out dinner, work for a while, then watch a DVD, agree upon an end time for the work. If one of you doesn't honor the end time, the other can understandably get upset. Even if you say, "Go ahead and start the DVD without me," he may resent that you didn't honor your agreement. If you really just need a few more minutes, negotiate for that, but then don't push your luck by going beyond. And unless you've been dating a while, don't try to multitask by watching the DVD and working on your laptop.

💜 ***Be sensitive to interrupting each other.*** My ex and I liked to read sitting next to each other. We'd often read something that we thought would be of interest to the other. So we developed a simple code: "Tell me when you're interruptible." This was not enough to bring you out of what you were reading, or if writing you could complete your thought. When we came to a stopping place — usually within a minute or two — we'd turn to the other and say, "I'm interruptible now" and we could share what was interesting.

> *"Tell me when you're interruptible."*

💜 ***Let the other know if something isn't working.*** If he interrupts you every few minutes, that won't work. I had a working date with a guy who talked to himself out loud. This was very distracting as I didn't know if he was talking to me specifically, or just thinking aloud. Finally, I said, "I like that we're working in the same room, but if we're going to continue, I need to ask you to not vocalize your thoughts unless you are talking to me." He understood.

💜 ***Decide how much you will tap the other for
input.*** I dated a former newspaper editor, so I'd
ask for his opinion when I was in a quandary
about a word choice or was struggling with how
to phrase something. But I made sure to not do
this often as he was working on his own stuff.

Have you had working dates? If so, what have you
found works?

My phone's not ringing. Is that you not calling?

My pal Manslations.com writer Jeff Mac wrote about how to get a man you're seeing to call you instead of just texting, IMing and emailing. He had some good wisdom about how we often think the other has the same preferences as we do, so we don't think of doing anything differently.

Honesty — what a concept!

Jeff wisely suggests being honest (honesty — what a concept!) about your desire to talk on the phone. He said to try, "I notice that you don't seem to be into making phone contact."

I felt compelled to comment:

> *My only tweak would be instead of "I notice that you don't seem to be into making phone contact" I'd say something like "I notice we don't talk on the phone. I like chatting live periodically. Would it be OK with you if we talked on the phone every few days?"*
>
> *The reason for the suggestion is the "I notice that you..." puts the onus on him — that it's his responsibility for calling. And it hints at blame that he hasn't called. I hate it when someone says "I haven't heard from you in a while." What — are your fingers broken? You can't make the call if you want to talk?*

In any communication, whether in dating, work, or personal life, your word choice speaks volumes. A little word like "you" can be inclusive and persuasive or blaming and repelling. When you want someone to grant your request, be conscious of your word choice and work to eliminate words that could be interpreted the opposite of your intention.

And I'm sure you know this, but perhaps it will serve as a reminder: Use "I" messages whenever possible. "I'd like to talk on the phone more often," or "I love it when you call," rather than "You need to call me more often," or worse, "You never call." The latter are more likely to be off putting.

"How many sexual partners have you had?"

This is a deadly question to ask someone you're dating. Whatever he says will be wrong. If he's had fewer than you think is appropriate, you'll think he's inexperienced. If he's had more — perhaps way more — than you think is acceptable, you'll think he's a slut.

And what if he asks you? Same problem. There is no way to answer this early in the relationship without some judgment being made, until you've been together for a while and can share this information without fear of judgment.

Does it matter how many notches are on your bedpost?

At a party a midlife, never-married woman shared she'd had 60 lovers. Some of the rest of us couldn't remember the count, as some were long ago in college. She had made a list.

Does it matter how many notches are on your bed-post? People assume that the more lovers you've had, the more experienced you are at various ways to please your partner. What if you had only one or two but learned a lot?

My suggestion: Don't ask, don't tell. If your date asks you, skirt around it with something like, "Enough to know how to make my partner happy." That could apply even if there was only one.

What do you think of this question? How have you responded when asked? And if you've been the one asking, what did you think when you heard his number?

When should you disclose any, er, unusual preferences?

I was once contacted by a man who said in his profile that he was "slightly kinky." When I asked what he meant exactly, he said he'd explain in person. He was a perfect gentleman on the phone and in emails, so I thought it was worth a coffee meeting to find out. I've learned that one person's kinky can be another's normal, so I decided not to worry too much about it until he explained. During our coffee date, he elaborated that he was a cross dresser on occasion. Okey dokie.

But another man didn't even hint at his unconventional preferences until an email nearly a week after our initial lunch. We'd had a dozen emails, phone conversations and IMs and nothing was even hinted at beforehand. I know people share his sexual practices, but I've not met anyone personally who told me they did. So I'm thinking that this man should have placed an ad on kinky.com or something similar, not Yahoo!Personals.

However, an acquaintance who is into swapping has an ad on Yahoo! Personals, as well as more provocative sites. He sent me his profile to read and he thought he was being explicit about his practices. He wrote that he was "adventurous" but he didn't say "sexually adventurous." He thought "adventurous" was enough. I thought it meant he liked to rock climb or participate in outdoor adventures. He said he told women from Yahoo!Personals on their first coffee meeting that he attended swapping parties. I told him I'd feel duped if he waited until then to disclose such an important element of his life that would affect many women's decision to meet him or not. I'd be irritated if I got dolled up and drove to a coffee meeting, then learned of his practice that I don't support and wouldn't date someone who did.

He wrote that he was "adventurous" but he didn't say "sexually adventurous."

I felt a bit hoodwinked myself by the man who didn't share his out-of-the-ordinary practices. I'd spent some time getting to know him and was interested in a second date. But I don't share a proclivity for the experiences he described. And I doubt I'd learn to like those kind of activities.

When should one disclose such alternative tastes? I

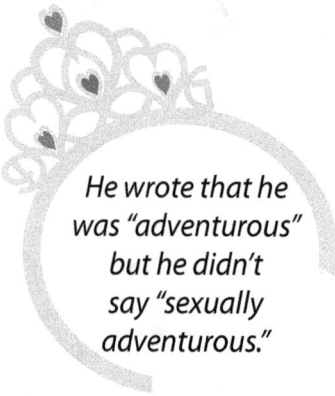

think you are beholden to at least hint at it in your profile or initial email, as the first man did. Did the second man think that I'd become so enamored with him that I'd ignore my own values? Did he think he'd scare off women if he shared earlier? He was just postponing the inevitable, but taking up someone's time in the process.

When do you think someone should disclose any practices that they know others may find off-putting?

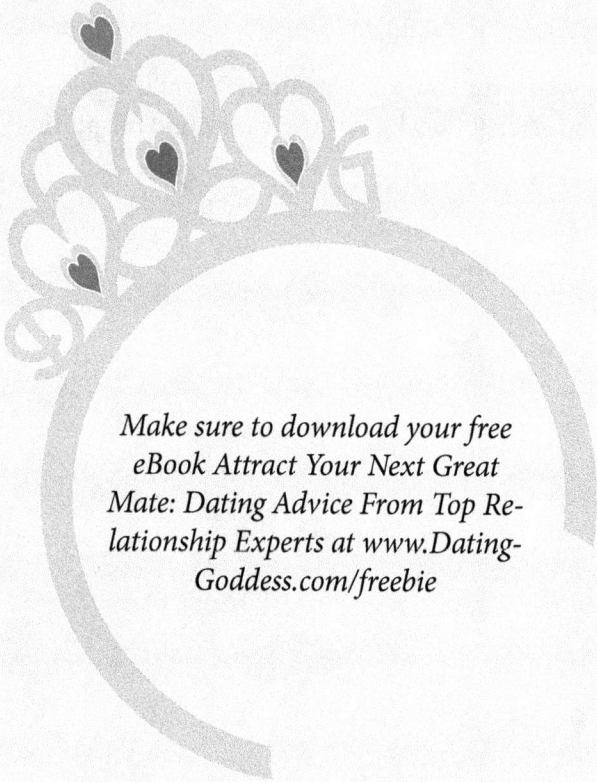

Make sure to download your free eBook Attract Your Next Great Mate: Dating Advice From Top Relationship Experts at www.Dating-Goddess.com/freebie

The faux vacation fling

You had an instant, magical, mutual connection. On the first date you both expressed how attracted you were to the other, and how much you enjoyed your time together. He kissed you on the cheek during dinner, showing that he was a gentleman — not assuming privileges too soon.

After dinner, neither of you wanted the date to end, but the restaurant was closing. You didn't want to say goodnight just yet. The waitress suggested a bar for "mature people" which you interpreted as anyone over 30. You struck out in pursuit of a place to linger with some unobtrusive dance music. The suggested tavern had morphed into a hard-rock, under-30 place. You found a nearby lounge at a chain restaurant, so you cozied up in a booth for more time together until it, too, closed.

You couldn't wait for the first kiss. It was as yummy as you'd hoped. You said goodbye for the evening. He promised to call the next day. He did. He called every day for the next four days, when you saw each other again. The hours passed quickly as you hung out, enjoying holding hands, talking, and sweet kisses. No pressure to go beyond simple affection — he wasn't pressing for sex. More expression of your both feeling close to each other. At the end of the evening, you felt you'd found someone with whom you could spend the rest of your life. Yes, you realize this was happening quickly and knew your friends would tell you to slow down, but you hadn't felt like this in years.

He called the next day and the next and the next. But there was no definite time set to get together. You called him and asked about lunch or dinner, but there was always some reason he couldn't set a day and time — meetings, business dinners, evening classes, short business travel. Was he in a relationship and just trying you out to be his spare? Had he changed his mind about how he felt? Had he been feeding you lines? Was he a player? If so, he would have pressed more for sex.

You toy with getting angry and telling him off. But you don't really know what's going on. He does call, so you think he's still interested. You struggle to not take it personally. He never really said he's finished; he's just not making an effort to get together again. But he does still stay in touch. You're tempted to cut the cord, but decide there's no loss with staying the course.

This has happened before, where things began swimmingly, deliciously, fabulously, only to have the connection dissipate. You can blame him for whatever (being a coward, leading you on, apparently lying, being uncommunicative), but that doesn't really get you anywhere. You could blame yourself (easily wooed, heart on your sleeve, needy, see things as you'd like them not as they really are, you get your hopes up too quickly), but that doesn't get you anywhere either.

I've decided that when I have these fizzled encounters — which luckily are rare — I will reframe them as vacation flings. So what if I wasn't really on vacation, or if these assignations happened within 25 miles of my house. A vacation fling is full of juicy romance, yet you know it is unlikely to continue when you return home. The difference between a real vacation fling and a faux, close-to-home one is with the former you know going in that it isn't going to last. With the latter you have to reframe it in retrospect — rewriting a bit of emotional history. Delusional? Perhaps. But it's harmless.

Does it still sting? It can. Or, just like with a vacation dalliance, you can look back with a smile, enjoy the connection and affection, and be happy you experienced it. After all, he wasn't abusive or mean, he was just not there for the long term — that being more than two weeks.

Have you experienced reframing a short, strong connection in a way that leaves you happy, not angry or hurt? If so, how did you recategorize the "relationship"?

Being played by a pathological liar

I think of myself as a good judge of character, just as nearly everyone I know thinks they are. I usually trust my gut and can often feel when something isn't right. If something doesn't make sense, I question it. While I generally trust people and look for the good in them, I am also skeptical. I am not easily fooled.

But he did it. He spun plausible stories, so even when his explanations were a tad over the top they seemed believable. He even admitted things sounded crazy. His voice was so convincing, I decided he would have to be a very good actor if what he was telling me wasn't true.

He was. It turned out he was a practiced liar. So much so, his family members repeatedly encouraged him to get psychological help.

How do I know? After talking to him daily for nearly a month, going out on a few dates and his expressing his deep connection to me, I didn't hear from him for a few weeks. The last time we spoke he said he'd call me back in an hour. He didn't. I became concerned about him. A week before that last conversation, he'd totaled his car and was in the hospital for a few days. I was worried that he might have had a complication and was back in the hospital.

I left him a few voice mails and emails trying to see if he was okay. When I didn't hear back, I imagined him in a hospital bed. I knew where his sister worked and that they talked frequently, so I finally braved calling her to see if he was all right. She was sympathetic and helpful.

"My brother is one of the nicest guys you'll ever meet. But he is not all that he has led you to believe."

"What do you mean?"

"He embellishes and fabricates."

"He lies?" I wasn't surprised, just wanted to confirm.

"Yes."

We went through the things he had told me. Some were true, others weren't, and some she wasn't sure about. Yes, he owned a Lexus as he told me, but she didn't know about the SUV he supposedly owned and rolled. She hadn't heard he had been in accident

"He embellishes and fabricates."

in the last month, even though they talked just last week. She confirmed he wasn't married and didn't have a girlfriend. When I asked what he really did for a living, she said what he told me is what he had told their mother, but they weren't really sure. Yes, the story he shared about his past girlfriend was true. But the cousin he told me died in his arms was still alive. And she had no knowledge of his being offered or taking a job out of state. He is really eleven years younger than he told me.

I shared with her, "I found a listing on the Internet in his name in his town for a driver's license suspension in 2004. He denied it was him."

"That was him."

"Odd thing to lie about."

The things he lied about were strange. People usually lie to get out of something and/or to present themselves as someone they aren't. So why would he lie about his cousin's death and the age difference between us? I can see why he might lie about the job, but he spun an elaborate tale about that.

"My mother, father and I have all told him he needs to get psychological help for his lying. He hasn't sought any. He learned to lie at an early age as a way to survive in our tough childhood neighborhood. Now there's no reason to lie, but he still does it. We don't know if he's bored and this makes life more interesting, or why he does it. We don't believe most of what he tells us until we have proof."

While I felt foolish to be duped, I was actually relieved to get answers. I like mystery movies, and when the riddle isn't solved cogently, it's unsettling. My feelings for this man had dissipated but I wanted to close the book having some questions resolved. Don't we wish every man who says or does something that doesn't make sense had such a forthcoming sister to tell us the truth?

Paying for the sins of predecessors

M en have told me it isn't fair when a women judges them based on behaviors of previous suitors. Ideally we all want to be assessed as individuals, not lumped into "men do this" or "women do that" stereotypes.

Yet it is difficult to not take into account past lessons from collective experiences with the opposite gender. After enough data points, you see patterns emerge. Of course there are always exceptions, but you begin to feel you can predict actions or at least be aware of common behaviors that are yellow or red flags.

> *It is difficult to not take into account past lessons*

A potential suitor and I were bantering recently and after he uttered a bawdy comment he added, "What can I say? I'm a guy and I'm horny." To which I responded,

"That's redundant."

Did I mean that all guys are horny? Of course not. But if a guy is in the dating world, my collective experience is that they are horny or lonely or a combination of both. Which is why they are dating!

With a new guy I am somewhat cautious, as I don't know much about his values, beliefs and behaviors. He could be a gem or a monster. So I'm a tad guarded. Is this fair to a man who has only honest intentions and is upfront about them? Is it right to be a bit suspicious even when there is no apparent need to be?

As women, we know it is better to be safe than sorry. We have learned that some men have only one thing on their mind!

When his hand is on
your knee too soon

An Adventures in Delicious Dating After 40 reader asks:

I just had a second date with a man who, during the show, put his hand on my leg. I removed it. To me that is way more intimate than holding hands or a hug — the kind of intimate "owning" thing that a serious other does — not someone I don't know at all.

This has happened to me on the first date! On one level, you could be flattered that he felt so comfortable with and attracted to you he behaved as if you've been dating longer. Or you could be incensed that he was so presumptuous and ungentlemanly that he would think this was okay.

Yes, most of us would be in the second camp.

You did the right thing to remove it. If you wouldn't be disturbing others around you, I would have also said, "We aren't at that stage in our relationship yet."

That said, on a first date, I said to the man, "If we were further along in our relationship, then I'd massage your aching shoulder." He said, "Well, then let's get further along," and started passionately kissing me, with little leading up to that. Ugh.

Back to you. Removing his hand and saying something without sounding pissy is important if you want to see him again. If you don't, then let him have it and leave. But I find gentle but firm works well if you want to salvage anything. A lot of midlife guys haven't dated a lot since their divorce, breakup or death of their mate (of course many have). If they haven't dated much, their model is when they dated in high school or college. So they are much more aggressive than the situation warrants.

Do you project life with your date?

Do you project your life into the future with the guy you've just started dating — sometimes even before you've met? I've been guilty of this, as well as been on the receiving end.

Let me give you some examples:

♥ I had a first coffee date with an award-winning professor at a local internationally renowned university. I knew he lived on campus, so I had already imagined what life would be like if I were to join him permanently. How delightful it would be to walk to the campus cultural events, lunch with visiting luminaries, and schmooze with world-famous lecturers.

♥ After one visit to a wealthy man's home, I began to fantasize my life if we were to become a couple. I mentally claimed his rumpus room for my office, and imagined which furniture I'd keep and what I would move. Could I rent out my house when I moved into his with the beautiful view?

When I briefly dated the Academy Award winning special-effects producer, I imagined attending private screenings, hobnobbing with the stars. On Oscar night, we'd get dolled up, then be swamped with photographers exiting the limo onto the red carpet. I'd be able to recreate his story of sipping martinis with Meryl Streep in the basement bar of the Kodak Theatre.

Do you do this? Or am I weird? If you, too, fantasize life with a guy you barely know — or haven't even met — why do you think we do this? Is it to explore one scenario of how life might be if we were to become an item? Is it to "test drive" a lifestyle? In my imagination, I don't foresee the drudgery — cleaning house, cooking meals, etc. I only focus on the positive or glamorous aspects. Is this expressing a romanticized vision of a potential life together, knowing that life is never comprised of only stellar moments? Are we setting ourselves up for disappointment since life with another has downs as well as ups?

Do you fantasize life with a guy you barely know?

I've been on the receiving end when a beau imagined getting a job in my area and moving in with me

— without my asking him! Another sweetie was ready to move in his coffee maker after the first sleepover. He also declared that he would not live with me in my house, that we'd sell my house and buy a new one together. So it seems both genders partake in forecasting a future together.

I asked a dating pal if she does this too, and when she assured me she does, I knew I wasn't alone in this behavior.

Boyfriend points

ow does a man earn "boyfriend points" with you? Does he get points when he calls, takes you out, says nice things, brings you flowers? How about opens the door, helps with your coat, takes you to your favorite restaurant, compliments you, plans fun activities? Or acts with integrity, is kind to strangers, pets dogs and cats, and makes you laugh?

"What's your date's Delight/Disappointment Scale score?" (page 17) shared how to track how you felt after and in between dates with a guy. We also explored this concept in "Tracking your date's score" (in the *First-Rate First Dates: Increasing the Chances of a Second Date* book) but didn't assign specific point values. Boyfriend points are in the same ball park, but slightly different.

John Gray says that a man gets points for each thoughtful thing he does for his woman. He says that instead of bringing his wife a dozen roses, he brings her one at a time over a series of days. Then he gets points for each act, whether it's one rose or a dozen. It's John's opinion that a man gets a point, in essence, for each demonstration that he was thinking of his woman and wanted to do something that pleased her.

One of my beaus liked to gather boyfriend points. He didn't ask what an individual act earns, but mentioned that he wants to earn as many boyfriend points as possible. If he did something that he thought I wouldn't like, he asked if he'd lost points.

One of my beaus liked to gather boyfriend points

Interestingly, if a man has banked enough points, the minor challenges don't really affect the bank account. He has earned grace with his steady thoughtfulness, kindness, and demeanor. So on the Delight/Disappointment Scale there would be a straight line, not a dip, even though the act wasn't a positive one. So if he occasionally walks in front of you, goes through the door first, doesn't help you with your coat, it's no big deal, as he nearly always does. No loss of points since it's a rarity.

I haven't figured out how many points are earned by what acts. I know what behaviors I like, so they get points, but all acts don't earn the same number of points. Maybe collectively we need to come up with a point guide so guys will know what will earn and cost them points, as well as how many. So, for example, if he's 20 minutes late and doesn't call, that costs him 10 points. But bringing you flowers earns him 20 points, so he's made up for it. Of course, we'd all have differ-

ent point assignments since we all value an act differently. But we could come up with a list and suggested
point values, then each woman could adjust it based
on her preferences.

What are some acts that earn points in your book,
and how many points would you assign specific acts? Of
course, the guys could come up with their own version.

"Ninny-ness"

A gal pal says that when you're enamored, smitten, enraptured, enthralled, and/or mesmerized with someone, you become a ninny. Your brain is not fully engaged. You do and say things to or with that person that if you were advising someone else, you'd tell him/her not to do/say. But you find yourself thinking these are perfectly reasonable things to do, or you hear words, phrases and questions fall out of your mouth before engaging your brain. This ninny-ness is confined to when you are speaking to the objet d'amore — otherwise you're fully functioning to others.

Ninny-ness is confined to when you are speaking to the objet d'amore

I was captivated by a charming, sexy man. After knowing him only a few weeks, and our expressing our strong mutual attraction, one day I heard myself blurt out on the phone, "Do you love me?" Arrgh! I immediately knew that was a stupid, stupid, stupid thing to say at this juncture. We'd only known each other a short while, how would anyone know if they loved the other? I tried to backpedal by saying, "That was a stupid question. Just ignore it." But it was like trying to ignore the streaker at the ball game — it was already out in full view. It sounded so needy, so clingy, so lame. Ugh!

Early in my post-divorce dating life I was bewitched by a man who lived less than a mile from me. I found myself driving out of my way to go by his house when doing errands. What — was I suddenly back in high school? When I snapped out of it and saw how juvenile this was, I stopped.

Have you experienced ninny-ness in your dating life? When you saw yourself being a ninny (during or afterwards), what did you catch yourself doing? How did you learn to stop it (if you did!)?

Easy way to ask hard questions

Some people find it difficult to ask probing questions to uncover their date's values, beliefs and preferences. Enter *Intellectual Foreplay: Questions for Lovers and Lovers To Be*, a book designed to help you easily dive into potentially difficult conversational waters.

The book is designed to be used by both of you. It is broken up into topic-focused chapters, with a strong warning not to start with the sex chapter! I used it with several men.

> *This book is designed to be used by both of you*

I've found it makes it really easy on car trips or sitting on the couch to say, "Let's dip into a few *Intellectual Foreplay* questions."

We taken turns choosing and answering questions. No matter what the question, you both answer it. I especially liked, "What attracts you to your partner?" There are questions on communication, hobbies, entertainment, morals, values, ethics, trust, romance, religion, health, money, work, family, food, vacations, and of course, sex.

The authors suggest you can either go through all the questions in a chapter, or choose specific questions from a section, or just open the book and randomly pick one. You can do this in person or on the phone. I'd suggest not doing it via email or IM as the person's voice tone tells you a lot. So ideally, you're in person, facing each other so you can see the other's body language.

I don't know that I'd bring this book to a first date, but I have shared the concept with someone over the phone and asked if he'd be interested in discussing a some of the questions. I cherry-picked a few I wanted to discuss and it went well. The key is you both answer the same question so I offered to go first to reduce it feeling like an interview.

The authors, Eve Eschner Hogan and Steve Hogan, used this technique to deepen a long-distance relationship and determine if they were truly compatible. As you can gather by their names, they got married, and they say it is because they got to know each other so well.

Examining your
concessions

When you've been with someone for a while, you've made compromises based on his preferences. In a healthy, nurturing, loving relationship, each person makes some adjustments to better get along with or please our partners.

If you've been together for years, these concessions become habits. You may not realize you even do them for him anymore. They seem like your way of doing things.

Only after the breakup, you may begin to notice — then question — these activities. I think it's a turning point in your moving on when you

1) become aware that you are doing something that would not be your preference, and

2) choose to do it differently or not at all.

My epiphany around this concept came months after my ex left. I was reading the morning comics, as is my habit. But when I came to Rex Morgan, M.D., I realized I had no interest in the strip. However, I read it for years, at the request of my ex — he liked it and wanted to discuss the story lines with me. It was no big deal to take 30 seconds each morning to catch up on the exploits of Rex, et al, and if it would please my husband, of course I'd do it. And we did regularly discuss it, so it wasn't for naught.

However, when he was no longer around, I realized I could stop doing something I did solely for him. I gleefully ceased reading the strip.

I began to look at other habits I'd established out of wanting to please him or keep calm in the house. Not that he was overbearing in any way. In fact, he was just the opposite. He didn't ask much of me, so when he did make a request, I was happy to oblige, as he often did to mine.

Have you examined elements of your life since your last long-term relationship? Have you looked at what TV shows you watch, which side of the bed you sleep on, what clothes you wear, what foods you buy and decided if those are really your preferences, or just what you did to please your man or keep the peace?

Compromise is not a bad thing, as long as it is equal. But after he's gone it's liberating to realize that what you've conceded doesn't have to stay that way and you can have your life any way you want it. Until your next relationship. But at least you are now starting from what you want, not what your ex liked.

The trophy beau

When a trophy wife or girlfriend is mentioned, it is often with derision and cattiness. We think of a beautiful but often empty-headed woman attached to a rich, powerful, often older, unattractive man.

But what if you're dating an attractive man? Not just a man you think is attractive, as we know a man's attractiveness to us increases based on how he treats us and how we feel about him. But a man who others say is handsome, good looking, or even hot?

> *My friends asked why I looked so happy and I whipped out a pic of my beau*

I had this experience last week when I was at my professional association convention. My friends asked why I looked so happy and I whipped out a pic of my beau. The most common response was, "Wow! He's handsome." Perhaps some were just being nice, but if a friend shows you a picture of an average-looking man, you are likely to mutter, "He looks like a nice man," or "He has a kind face." But you are not inclined to give his looks a higher rating than you feel.

So after a dozen reactions to his striking good looks, I felt compelled to add, "And he's highly intelligent, extremely thoughtful, and treats me like a queen." I didn't want my friends thinking I was enamored with him only because he is hot. I felt obliged to let them know he was more than eye candy.

Not that I was apologizing for having a stunning beau. But I wanted my pals to know that I loved more about him beyond his looks.

Have you dated a gorgeous man who others recognized as such? If so, did you find yourself wanting to explain he had virtues deeper than his handsome features and/or buff body?

"Whip appeal" pros and cons

A man I dated for a while expressed his attraction to me in an interesting way: "You have whip appeal."

Huh? I've heard of men being "whipped" by their woman, and it is not a thing most men would admit to. In fact, a man's pals may tease him about being "whipped" if he seems too besotted by his woman.

In my quest to understand this term I learned it is from Babyface's song titled "Whip Appeal" in which he exclaims, "no one but you has that kind of whip appeal on me." This sounds like a good thing — at least to me!

I took my inquiry to some young men friends. When I told a gal pal's 21-year-old son what my guy said, he responded, "Congratulations!" He explained that this is a very good thing. My man was saying he was so attracted to me I had him wrapped around my finger and he was fine with it. Cool!

Another friend's twenty-something son got a big smile as he explained. "It means a woman is so wonderful the man can't stop thinking about her and how to make her happy." Good again!

How do you know you have whip appeal? I've learned a man can say things like this that lead you to believe he is totally into you. But you need to pay attention to not only what he says but what he does. This man was masterful at saying the right thing, and when we were together he treated me well. When we were apart he'd text me daily love notes, but did little else to give me what I told him I needed. So while "whip appeal" may have some allure, make sure there is consistency in his application of this concept.

While I don't want a man I can push around, knowing he is irresistibly drawn to you isn't bad. Unless, of course, it's a one-dimensional attraction and then a deal breaker surfaces in that arena. Your whip appeal will disappear so quickly you get whiplash!

Have you become exclusive too soon?

Y ou've been dating a man for 2 months. There have been some issues to work out, but generally you really like the man. A discussion of exclusivity comes up. You each share what you need from a relationship to be exclusive and the other agrees to try to provide it, or if you know you can't make meet a need, you say so. You both decide you'd really like to focus on each other and not date others. You agree to only see each other and remove your profiles from any dating sites.

A few weeks pass and your man is making some attempts to provide what you say you need, but the effort is inconsistent. You rack it up to he's trying and you don't expect perfection. But you aren't consistently getting enough of what you want and you're feeling disappointed.

You share this with him. He promises to try harder. Which he does for a few days, then slacks off to old habits. You wonder if you should give up some of your needs as they seem so difficult for him to provide, or if you should keep reminding him. He seems sincere in his interest to give you what you want.

Another week or two pass. You realize he isn't really trying to provide what you need. You like being with him so don't want to cut it off, but you are left without some critical needs being met. You realize you'd really like to date other men, especially a few you'd met right before you decided to become exclusive with this man. You think they might be a better fit for you.

You realize you've agreed to be exclusive too soon. You could renegotiate, telling him you'd like to date other people. But you know he feels strongly about monogamy, so you're doubtful he'd go for it. You either have to stick it out with him a while longer to see if he will make more effort to give you what you want, or break it off entirely.

The problem, you now see, is you agreed to exclusivity without enough evidence that he would provide what you want. You had it backwards and should have agreed to exclusivity only after you had certainty he was willing and able to meet your needs. You bet your heart based on faith. You said yes based on his promise, not on his demonstrating action first.

Before agreeing to exclusivity, communicate clearly what you want and need. Discuss if anything the other wants isn't possible or probable. Then wait for the consistent and prolonged demonstration of the promises, not just words. Only then should you enter into an exclusive relationship. Not before.

The stealth date

I went out with a delightful man three times while my last beau and I were broken up for a few weeks some months ago. When we decided to get back together, I told this man the news. Since we are in the same field and I liked his personality, I asked if we could stay in touch as pals. He said he'd like that.

Over the past 4 months we've talked for an hour every few weeks, taken several long walks together, and attended a professional meeting. I shared with him the final demise of my relationship with my beau, and we talked for an hour about what we've learned from past relationships. We laugh a lot, flirt some, and share our successes and setbacks.

Sounds like a great relationship, huh?

Agreed.

He is tall, sensitive, strong, funny, good looking, well dressed, intelligent, articulate, and well read. We are attracted to each other on several levels. So why am I not jumping back into a dating relationship with him?

Several reasons.

♥ I'm not sure I'm emotionally ready to invest in a new romantic relationship right now. This man has long-term potential, and my emotions are still a bit raw from the breakup. I'd hate to be needy or submit him to anger or disappointment that is really about my last beau, not him. While he is savvy enough to know when something is really about him or not, I'd hate to put him through that, or worse, destroy what we have while I'm healing.

In the past I've jumped into romantic relationships too quickly. I've gone from just meeting someone to holding hands or smooching on the second date if I was drawn to the guy. I need to do a better job of learning if a guy has the same values and how he treats me before progressing to a romantic relationship.

> I need to do a better job of learning if a guy has the same values

He's in between jobs. He quit his last job in March and hasn't found a new one. I've psychologically supported him in his mood management and job search, but it is a full-time job to find a job. Any relationship, especially a budding one, takes time and energy. I think he'd be best served to stay focused on getting a job.

So by hanging out and talking with this guy, it is stealth dating. We do things that cost little or no money, or go Dutch. I can see how he treats me as a person to get a sense of how he might treat me as a sweetie. I watch him interact with others. I can see how often he initiates contact and what he invites me to do. All of this without the messiness of being disappointed if he doesn't call every day or set up a date at least once a week. We are experiencing how we get along and when one of us wants to connect with the other, we call.

Isn't this how dating really should be? You get to know and like the other person before progressing? Sometimes I think the dating world starts a few steps down the road, when it really needs to start with "Do I like you? Do we have similar values and interests? Do I like how we interact? Do I think about you when we aren't together?"

We both know we're attracted to each other, but it feels right to step back a bit and hang out together to see if we want to progress.

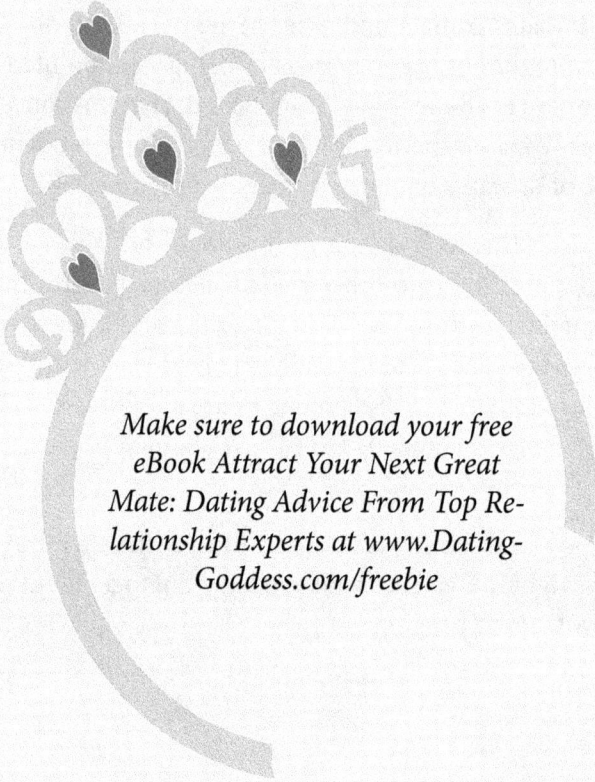

Make sure to download your free eBook Attract Your Next Great Mate: Dating Advice From Top Relationship Experts at www.Dating-Goddess.com/freebie

How is your guy imprinted on you?

When you are besotted by a guy you begin to associate him with t I need to do a better job of learning if a guy has the same values hings related to him. His cologne, style of shirts, favorite musical artists or songs, car make and color, even most-liked foods are imprinted in your brain as markers for him.

Which is great when things are going well. When you see something that reminds you of him, you smile and get a warm feeling. You encounter triggers that flash images of him several times a day and you remember his cute smile, loving embrace, or soft kiss.

The challenge is when he's broken up with you and you still have feelings of love or fondness toward him. You're trying to let him go, move on and push his memory to the back burner. But instead, you see reminders of him more frequently than you'd like. You find yourself getting emotional over everyday things and it's embarrassing to get teary eyed when you walk past a man who smells like him, wears the same brand and style of shirt, or hear his artist playing on the radio.

When I was with my last beau, I would commonly happen upon stimulus that reminded me of him and it would make me happy. However, after the break up, those same prompts would send me into an emotional tizzy. Soon after the dissolution of our relationship I saw a man wearing the same uniform my ex-beau wore in the pictures I repeatedly saw of him on the job. Even though I had actually never seen him wearing his uniform, the photos were indelibly seared into my memory. So much so that seeing this stranger in a similar uniform instantly elicited overwhelming sadness and tears.

> *After the break up, those same prompts would send me into an emotional tizzy*

In "It's moving day!" I encourage everyone who's experienced a breakup to get rid of any physical objects that remind you of your past love, no matter if it was you or he who broke it off. It is much easier to remove these memory joggers from your house than it is to close your eyes, ears and nose every time you see, hear or smell something outside your home that refreshes your memory of him. You have no control over what make or color of cars pass you, what musical artist is playing in Starbucks, or what cologne the man next to you on the plane is wearing.

You only have control over your reaction. But sometimes this can be the hardest thing to curb if you have etched in your psyche the connection of this stimulus to the man. It takes some consciousness and effort to sever the feelings from the trigger. It is said that time heals the wound, but if your emotions get triggered repeatedly, the wound keeps being ripped open. The more you can repeat that you were not a good match and release your feelings for him, the easier it will be to reduce the impact these triggers will have on you. And eventually they will have no effect at all. You will have broken the imprinted connection and you will be free to be open to someone new.

Rose-colored glasses obscure red flags

When you look through colored glass, it distorts the colors you see, especially colors in the same range. They are not as vivid as when you look through clear glass. The same is true in relationships. Rose-colored lenses diffuse red — especially red flags.

You are smitten. He is so perfect for you. He is not only everything on your list of the ideal man, he has many other bonuses too! He's got that great smile, long eyelashes, cute butt. He knows how to brighten your day with brief text messages, but not too many that feel smothering. You are head over heels for him — a goner!

So what if he never answers the phone when you call. Or he prefers long text messages to phone calls. He's so attentive when you're together, you'll overlook the little things. And you think that his leaving his cell phone in the car when you're together is a sign of how focused he wants to be on you, not wanting to be interrupted by anyone else.

And does it really matter that he calls and wants to see you in an hour, even though you've said several times you prefer a day's notice? He wants to see you and you him, so you reshuffle your work so you can make the time for him. His kisses and caresses are worth a little rearranging.

You don't even notice that your assignations are always on weekdays, never weekends. After all, you both have flexible schedules so does it really matter what day of the week you rendezvous — as long as you see each other?

You think it's kinda cute that he holds you tight and when you say you need to go get a drink of water he doesn't let go. He likes holding you — how sweet.

His always paying for dinners, movies, etc. in cash telegraphs to you that he isn't a slave to any credit card debt.

Isn't it gentlemanly that he always insists on making the drive to your house? And when you suggest you'd love to see his, he protests that it is way too messy to invite anyone to visit. He wouldn't want you to see what a pack rat he is and think poorly of him because of it.

He always insists on making the drive to your house

He isn't available to attend any of the social events you invite him to. You understand. He's a busy man with other commitments. And it doesn't strike you odd

that he never invites you to any of his family or social functions.

But then something happens and your rose-colored glasses are shattered. You then see that all these endearing examples were really covers for a controlling, self-focused, or even married man. And you made up interpretations of his behavior to match the man you wanted him to be. You were too gaga over him to see any of these red flags.

So be forewarned: when you find yourself besotted you will overlook glaring signs that he is not what you interpret him to be.

If his stories don't add up, subtract yourself

When we begin to date someone new, nearly always he is a stranger. Even if you meet through friends, work, class, church or other activities, you most likely barely know him. While you want to be open and trusting, you also want to be conscious of inconsistencies that point to him not being who he represents himself to be. It is hard to balance giving someone the benefit of a doubt with being overly suspicious.

But when his actions or stories don't add up, then take yourself out of the equation.

Here are some things that you should note, although singularly an item could mean nothing. But if there are a number of these, proceed very cautiously or extricate yourself altogether.

- His phone has caller ID blocked.

- His cell phone has an area code from another state although he says he's never lived there.

- He never answers his phone when you call. He calls you back minutes, hours or days later.

- He only calls you from his car or work, never home.

- He texts you long conversations rather than calling you.

- After months of dating, he's never invited you to his house.

- After two months of dating regularly, he hasn't introduced you to any of his friends.

- After several months of dating he won't give you his address.

- He prefers to bring take out to your house or have you fix dinner rather than take you out.

- You don't hear from him for several days even though you usually connect daily. When you finally do and ask what he's been up to, he is evasive about where he's been.

- He only wants to meet you for weekday lunches, not dinner.

- He professes to care for you deeply but repeatedly treats you disrespectfully or regularly ignores your desires.

- He lives nearby, is retired, and tells you daily how much he misses you but makes only minor efforts to see you.

- He only pays with cash for your activities.

Inconsistencies are how we tell if someone is untrustworthy. Most people either don't notice them or shrug them off. I have been guilty of noticing them but ignoring them if I liked a guy a lot. But that has caused a lot of pain as he's ended up taking me for a ride which I had indications was coming. And it was not a fun ride — more like a bucking mechanical bull. Getting bucked off something you knew wasn't real but pretended was is not only painful, but humiliating.

> *Inconsistencies are how we tell if someone is untrustworthy*

So don't ignore the signs that something is amiss. Keep your logic cap on and notice when something doesn't make sense. Ask about it with curiosity, not confrontation. If enough answers don't make sense, then move on. You need to be with someone you can trust explicitly, not always wonder if he's lying to you or not.

Reporting in or sharing your lives?

What is your preference for connection frequency once you begin to date a man regularly? Some people like daily chats, while some think that is onerous. And when you do connect, what do you both want to hear and share?

I've been surprised when this issue is a bone of contention. I think most of us have the self-centric assumption that we'd share similar preferences with someone to whom we're attracted. We may unfortunately eventually learn that attraction doesn't necessarily mean similar values, preferences, or perspectives.

In a communication after a breakup, I learned that my request for daily connection had been perceived by my ex-beau as a requirement for him to "report in." He was what I considered evasive and secretive about his activities when I really just wanted to have a sense of his life when we were apart. I explained to him that I perceived our daily contact as a chance to connect, not only by sharing what was happening in our lives, but taking it deeper by exploring our achievements, concerns, hopes and fears. He felt it was a requirement he report in and explain his whereabouts to me.

I think he had issues about this left over from his marriage. He'd told me that when he returned home from work his wife wanted to know what had happened during his day. His job was not particularly pleasant and he didn't want to relive the odious things with which he'd had to deal. So even after being out of that job for over a decade, he had no desire to share a recap of his daily life with me.

(In all fairness, I can understand having someone want to know your every action. My late mother would sometimes call and want to know the details of my day, down to what I had for lunch. I realized this was her way of wanting to connect with me and she didn't know how to take the conversation beyond the reporting-in level.)

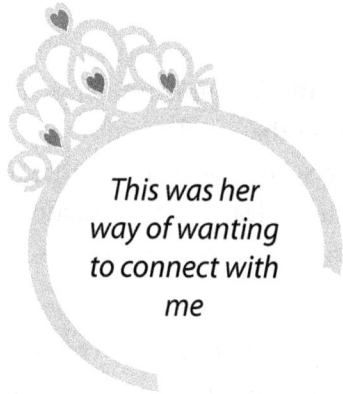

> *This was her way of wanting to connect with me*

One would think that this would be an easily resolved issue between two midlife people who have a desire to be together. But if you have opposite needs about this, it is a difficult one to resolve. And before this relationship, I wouldn't have guessed it would be so difficult to find a middle ground. The problem wasn't as much about contact frequency, as I would have been okay connecting every other day or so. But it was more the content of the communication that left me longing for connectedness. I felt it was like pulling teeth to hear about the highlight of his day, or important issues he faced, or even where he was. (He frequently stayed away from home overnight, he said at friends, but sometimes those friends were a 5-hour drive away and I had no idea he was gone.) He was so secretive I wondered if he was seeing one or more other women.

So if regular connection — not just a quick text message — is important to you, discuss this with your guy before getting too wrapped up in him. If he's not willing to share conversation about his life, he's probably not going to be willing to share his life with you.

Should you wait for the other to fall for you?

Adventures in Delicious Dating After 40 reader
Mark asks:

> How do you know if it's time to move on when you
> are enamored of the other person, but that person
> doesn't return those same feelings yet is still willing
> to stay in the relationship?

> My situation is that I really, really like this woman.
> She seems right for me. I'm very attracted to her,
> think about her all the time, gush to her in emails,
> and so on. I've been seeing her for nearly eight
> months, too, so it's not like these feelings are the
> initial rush of romance.

> She has feelings for me too and is attracted to me
> as well. However, she says she doesn't have the
> kind of feelings she would expect to have after this
> much time, and the thought of meeting someone
> else doesn't bother her, though she isn't interested
> in looking right now. She wonders if it's something

about where she is in her life right now rather than me, but she doesn't know. We are both in our late 40's and divorced.

I enjoy being with her and I really don't want to date anyone else, and the idea of going through the whole discovery process with someone new makes me feel tired rather than excited, so I feel like I'd like to ride things out with her. I also think that we could be happy together, though for her she might be settling if she decided to stay with me.

I really like her, though, so I feel like holding on as long as she lets me hold on. No relationship will ever be perfect, and it's entirely possible that she and I will never be in a better relationship than what we have right now.

There are a lot of bad dates out there waiting to happen. It's the imperfect bird in the hand versus who knows what is in the bush? two birds? no birds? lots of birds that are a waste of time?

Dear Mark:

Right now you are her Better Than Nothing guy — the common expression for a lopsided relationship. She likes hanging around with you, but is open to meeting someone else. When she does you'll be dropped into the "friend" category pronto. That will hurt. I understand part of your rationale: if it were me I'd be thinking, "We just need to hang around more for him to see what a fabulous person I am and fall in love with me." It could happen. The question for you is, how long are you going to wait? You could be in this limbo for years, not moving forward in the relationship, just hanging out, perhaps friends with benefits from her perspective.

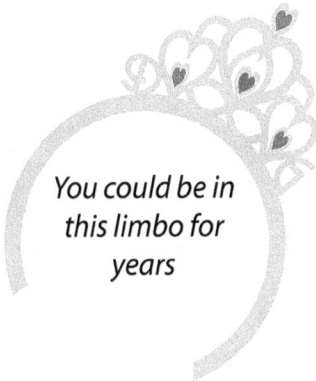

I know you aren't interested in dating someone else right now, but I'd encourage you to keep dipping in the pool. Two things might happen:

You could be in this limbo for years

You may meet someone who returns your feelings equally, or

She'll see you're not waiting around for her and aren't available anytime she wants so she may see what a great guy you are and those feelings of passion may get kindled.

But putting your life on the shelf while she is ambivalent isn't fair to you. You don't want to be with a woman who you fear might feel she settled. You will always be tiptoeing around, concerned that you will do something that will make her leave. You won't be able to be yourself as you would with someone who is equally committed to the relationship.

I know all too well how daunting it is to think of beginning the dating process again. Yes, there are many, many, many not great starts. And when you find someone who you really fancy, you want to give them as much room as they need to come around. So far — after going out with 112 men in 4 years — I've only got heartache from that wait. And wasted a lot of time in the process because I've taken myself out of the dating pool.

You deserve someone who thinks you are as magnificent as you think she is.

Signs of endearment — or just habits?

When we are fond of a man, we look for signs of his endearment toward us. We seek affirmation that he thinks as dearly about us as we do about him. Sometimes we mistake his natural habits for signs that he is going out of his way to show his affection toward us.

For example, you are on your third date and he:

♥ Has Country and Western music playing on his radio when he drives you to the restaurant. "Wow!" you think, "He must have remembered I like Garth Brooks and set the radio on Country because he knew I liked it."

♥ Takes you to a Thai restaurant without asking your preference. "How thoughtful he is," you tell yourself. "He remembered my mentioning my Thailand trip a few years ago and knew I'd like the food."

♥ Seats you at the table, walks on the outside of the sidewalk, opens doors for you, helps with your coat and insists that he come around to open the car door for you. You think, "How sweet that he is treating me like a queen. He must really like me."

The truth is, this is what he would do naturally, without thinking — or at least not necessarily thinking about you. These are his preferences or habits. He likes C&W music and Thai food. He has been trained since childhood to be chivalrous. None of these things are necessarily about his trying to please you or show his fondness toward you.

> *None of these things are necessarily about his trying to please you*

Of course, these could be indications of his enchantment. But many times we interpret behaviors like these as absolute signs when they aren't.

Now if he prefers reggae but plays C&W on the radio because he knows you like it, yes, he's showing his desire to make you happy. If he would rather have Chinese but knows you love Thai, then yes, he's showing his affection. If he normally wouldn't be conscious of where he walks but knows it makes you feel cherished if he walks on the outside, he's showing his care by doing what he knows you like.

In retrospect, I've interpreted simple acts as major signs that a man is entranced by me. When the rose-

colored glasses have come off, I saw that he was doing whatever he naturally did and I took it as a massive sign that he was into me. Of course, there were instances of him consciously doing what he knew I liked. But I've been sobered by the realization that so much of what I interpreted as beguilement and wooing was in fact just what he would do for any women in his presence, whether romantically interested or not. And often it was what he'd do if alone.

So be careful about what you make to mean a sign he's into you.

Notice who initiates ongoing communications

W omen know that if a man doesn't ask to spend time with her, he's not that interested in her. We have learned some men appreciate when a woman suggests a first date, but what about other communication?

If a woman initiates phone calls more often, she may tell herself, "He's too busy at work to think of calling. So I'll give him a jingle to see how he's doing."

If the woman is generally the one who starts email or text exchanges with a man, she may think, "He's just not much of an emailer/texter."

Recently I've become aware of a more subtle indicator: who initiates an IM most often. When a man asks if he can IM me and I accept, we can both see each other on our buddy list. When I'm online, I can see when he logs in and out, and he can see when I log in and out. I've often looked forward to seeing when a man who interested me logs in and I'd initiate the IM. Now I don't. I figure if he wants to say hello, he can see I'm online.

More often than not, I put myself in invisible mode, not allowing people to see I'm online. If I want to make myself available when I notice someone come online, I can. But mostly I don't.

Why?

Because that makes it too easy. I want a man who puts a little effort into our communication. If he can IM me w/virtually no effort, then he isn't really thinking about me, just bumping into me online. I prefer he actually decides he wants to talk to me and dials the phone.

Is this being a prima donna? Of course, I don't think so. To me a prima donna would NEVER initiate. I initiate some, but now I'm conscious of not doing most of it.

Why is this important? Because it's so easy to delude ourselves that someone is into us when really he is just responding to our overtures. I've been on the giving and receiving ends of this. I've had men contact me who didn't really interest me and yet I responded if he was nice. However, I've learned not to imply there is any romantic interest because I don't want them to misinterpret my niceness, and I don't want either of us to waste time. And early on, I'll suggest that we be friends.

By not initiating IMs, I am seeing how much interest a man really has in getting to know me. If I'm just a mouse-click away and he only IMs me, there's not much interest. If he at least picks up the phone and call, there is much more. It may seem like a little thing, but I've learned it takes Herculean effort for some men to call. In that case, how interested can he really be?

"Give me a raise and I'll work harder" applied to dating

This phrase doesn't work in a job. So why do people think this concept will work in dating?

For example, it appears common thinking is:

"I'll treat you like my girlfriend if we have sex."

"I'll be more affectionate to you after you treat me like a queen."

"I'll meet your family after we've hung out with my friends for months."

"I'll clean up my house after you move in."

I've fallen prey to this, thinking that if I gave a man what he wanted, he'd give me what I wanted. Unfortunately, solid relationships aren't built on tit for tat. They are built on "I want to give this to you because I know it makes you happy." Not "I will give you this if you give me that."

Of course every relationship involves some negotiation. "I'll attend your business dinner if you'll come to my friend's birthday party." Or, "I'll wear that dress you really like even if it's uncomfortable, if you take me to a nice restaurant."

It becomes problematic when you expect to get what you want only after you've given the other what he wants. He may give it to you, reluctantly. Or he may give it to you once to hold up his part of the bargain, but never again. Or he may not give it to you at all.

In the job scenario, we tend to get raises (or bonuses) after at least meeting expectations, and usually not until we've exceeded them. To tell your boss you'll work harder only after getting a raise will generate laughter, not trust. You have to demonstrate you are interested in getting a raise by working hard to show you deserve one.

The same should be true in budding relationships. You need to show you are interested in winning the other's heart and trust before getting them.

This seems like such common sense, but I'm continually surprised that even with midlife daters, it isn't.

What have you been surprised men you've been seeing expect without doing the work to show they deserve it?

Is he a weed or a wild flower?

I'm a gardener. Every year new flora grow in my garden that I didn't plant.

Some call these weeds. Others call them wild flowers. What you call them depends on your perspective.

While attending to some of these new residents in my garden, it reminded me of prospective suitors who come into our lives.

Women often classify men who have some flaw or who clearly aren't a match for them as "weeds." They treat these men with disdain for sullying their "garden" (the woman's life) by showing up in it. They want to get rid of them immediately as soon as they decide they don't want them around, without really knowing if they have something to offer.

Some weeds take great effort to get rid of. And others persistently keep showing up, even after you think you've ridden your garden of them.

However, wild flowers often delight you with their appearance and bring you joy with their existence. They are welcomed and treasured. Right now I have volunteer mini-pansies, sweet peas, morning glories, poppies, and Queen Anne's Lace interspersed in my garden, giving me a smile with their blossoms.

The terms "weed" and "wild flower" often refer to the same plant. It depends on your attitude about it.

A man who doesn't match your list of your perfect mate can be considered a weed, to be taken out of your life as quickly as possible. But if he delights you in any way, he should be considered a wild flower and treated with care.

Some of these men/wild flowers will become a permanent part of your garden/ life, giving you joy each time you encounter them. Some will not endure. Some will flourish with a little attention and encouragement. You will pull out those you realize don't really fit your plan. Some will get too pushy and try to take over your garden/life so you will prune them to what works for you, or eliminate them all together.

Some of these men/wild flowers will become a permanent part of your garden/ life

You will pull out some weeds immediately, like net-

tles that have sharp thorns and you know you don't want in your garden. You will keep some around for a while to see if you like them. And others will be with you for the long haul because you like what they provide.

So before you eliminate a man who isn't exactly what you expected, if he adds something to your life — he makes you laugh, is fun, invites interesting conversation — keep him around. He might not be a perennial, long-term mate, but instead become a special friend.

(BTW, in my garden I also have several non-wild flower volunteers — two tomato plants that are already setting fruit and a 6' peach tree with baby peaches! You never know when your volunteers will yield fruit for your table — or your soul.)

"You are perfect for me"

I was seduced by these words. They went straight to my heart. Even though the local man's actions rarely paralleled this sentiment. Much of the time I wondered why he didn't bother to set a time to get together while his text and phone messages talked about how much he missed me and cared about me. Why was I taken in by words that weren't backed by con-sistent action? Part of me longed to believe them. And frequently when we were together, I felt his ac-tions proved his words. But we saw each other maybe a day out of every 10 — 10% of the time.

> I wondered why he didn't bother to set a time to get together

When we were together he would look me in the eye while holding me close and say these words clearly — and I felt, sincerely. I so wanted them to be true.

And I was not without fault. I would say them back to him even though I was often frustrated — sometimes even angered — by his lack of initiative to see me and his sometimes disrespectful behavior. My logical mind knew he was far from perfect for me. But my heart was taken in by his words — coupled with my desire to believe them. When I said them back to him, at that moment I believed them.

Now I've learned to be more skeptical. The words are heart melting when you hear them. But you have to make sure they are backed by consistent, congruent behavior that shows he feels you are perfect for him. Otherwise they are just air.

Of course, part of you knows the words are expressing happiness with the other, knowing perfection in a relationship is rare. But you don't listen to that voice. You only listen with the ear of romance, wanting to believe you can be perfect for someone, even if you know he is not really perfect for you. And truthfully, you don't really believe you are perfect for him as you don't see the actions that reinforce that.

What words have you learned not to trust when not backed by congruent behaviors? ("I love you," "I adore you," "I'd never hurt you" come to mind.) What have you uttered that your mind knew wasn't true, but your heart felt was true at the moment?

Table manners: Knife and death at dinner

I've heard men say that women are too picky about unimportant aspects of a man's behavior. I think it depends on what one considers important and unimportant.

Many women would consider table manners important (or somewhat important). Few of us appreciate a man who chews with his mouth open, talks with his mouth full, licks his knife or lowers his head near the plate to more easily shovel food into his maw. Yet men who have these behaviors haven't a clue they are important, and would probably rebuff anyone pointing out their bad manners.

Yet for women, this can be a deal breaker with a man who hasn't ingratiated himself to her. If she is on the fence about a guy, his table manners can be the kiss of death — the only kiss that will be present that evening.

Last night is a case in point. The guy was pleasant, nothing glaringly wrong, although he seemed to have some difficulty finding topics to discuss. I drew him out and shared relevant information. Dinner arrived. He cut off large chunks of his chicken parmesan and stuffed them into his mouth as he continued to talk. The spaghetti, which is hard to eat gracefully under any circumstance, was consumed via large forkfuls, then protruding stands slurped in. This was punctuated with large draughts of bottled beer.

Our potential romantic partnership fell to the other side of the fence — with a thud.

I wondered — briefly — if I was being snobbish to not be enamored with uncouth table manners. I decided, no, that my partner must be someone with whom I can feel comfortable in polite company. Not that I attend society balls, but I do dine with bank-president clients and worldly friends and colleagues. I can't be with someone whose table manners are embarrassing.

In the past, some beaus' dining etiquette was so bad it elicited comments from my family members after the event. One licked his knife in a white-tablecloth restaurant. I don't relish making excuses for loutish behaviors.

If you chew with your mouth open or talk with your mouth full, stop. If you don't know which water glass or bread plate is yours at a table for 8, get educated. It's really not hard — information is easily available. Or maybe you don't know you're doing something others would find oafish. Ask someone who you think would know proper manners and get their discrete feedback.

Are you expecting boyfriend behavior too soon?

Sharing with a gal pal after a second date, I expressed disappointment that my date didn't treat me like my last beau did. My wise friend said, "You're expecting him to display boyfriend behavior but he's not your boyfriend yet." She was right! In fact, he probably hadn't even decided he was interested in being my boyfriend.

While we can expect men we're beginning to date to be courteous and hopefully chivalrous, some behaviors are more along the lines of "taking care of my woman." Some very chivalrous men behave this way for any woman they know. Others have more of a hierarchy, ascending to the next level as he becomes more fond of her.

Men have shared that when in a relationship, they adopt an attitude of protection toward the woman. They are more concerned that she's made it home safely, her home is secure and her car won't break down. They check in with her regularly to make sure if she has any upset he can fix, he will do his darndest.

When just getting to know a woman, a conscientious man will walk a woman to her car, help her on and off with her coat, and open doors. While this shows he cares, these behaviors can also be so engrained he does them for nearly any woman he accompanies, regardless of his romantic interest in her.

I notice when men display these behaviors and appreciate them, but I've now learned not to take them as signs a man has feelings for me. It seems each man has different baseline behaviors he displays from the first date and then adds to them as he feels more connection.

> *I've now learned not to take them as signs a man has feelings for me.*

So if you interpret early behaviors as expressing his attraction to you, you can be disappointed to find that's how he acts toward all women he's getting to know.

As your relationship deepens, what if he doesn't display the boyfriend behaviors you'd like? Of course, you can make requests and if he's astute he will pick up what you like. So instead of getting angry that he doesn't do something you want, you can ask him directly, then tell him how much you appreciate it.

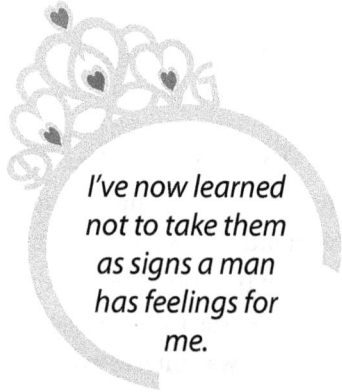

For example, you are chilly in the over-air conditioned movie theater, having left your wrap in the car. Don't just complain how cold it is and expect he'll offer to get your sweater. Instead ask, "Sweetie, would you be a dear and get my sweater from the car while I hold the seats?" If he's into you, he will jump at the opportunity to show you he can take care of you. And when he gets back, make sure to say, "Thank you. I appreciate your taking care of me this way."

Guess what? Next time you say you're cold, he'll probably offer to get your coat from the car. If not, just gently ask him. You are training him to display boyfriend behavior that you appreciate. And make sure you acknowledge him when he does what you like. We all like to be acknowledged and if we care about the person, we learn what they like by what they thank us for.

What do you consider boyfriend behavior that you wouldn't expect early on?

Have you ever been disappointed that someone didn't display boyfriend behavior when just starting to date?

"You are the best thing that ever happened to me"

At my 25-year-old friend's wedding a few weeks ago, I marveled at not only how elated the couple looked, but also how the parents beamed. As a friend of the groom's family, I was privy to how they really felt about their new daughter-in-law.

The couple met four years ago. The groom had been adrift, unsuccessful in college and spending the winter working at a ski slope and enjoying his ski bum life-style. That changed when they became a couple. She helped him articulate his dreams, set goals, and reenroll in community college, along with her. They got an apartment together and both got jobs. He raised his previously flunking grades to A's, which allowed them to transfer to a university.

When they got engaged, his mother said to me, "She is the best thing that ever happened to him."

I thought this when I watched the merry couple at the wedding. It reminded me of my now ex-brother-in-law telling me he'd scolded my ex (his brother) when told he'd left me. My brother-in-law (bless his heart) chastised my ex, telling him: "She's the best thing that ever happened to you. You'd be an idiot to leave her."

I realized my ex never told me I was the best thing that ever happened to him. I don't think he believed that. In fact, I doubt now he'd consider me or our marriage in the top 20. It made me ponder how our relationship might have been different if we regularly said that to each other, assuming we believed it. I had bouts of believing he was the best thing to ever happen to me, but to be honest, it was rare.

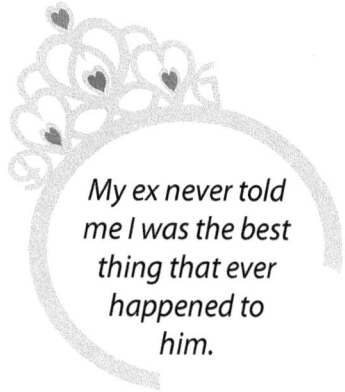

> *My ex never told me I was the best thing that ever happened to him.*

At the post-wedding brunch, I pulled the newly-weds aside separately. I said, "Would you like one idea that will help you have a long, loving and successful marriage? Tell the other every day, 'You are the best thing that ever happened to me.' Not just 'I love you' — that is important — but also tell him/her how important s/he is to you. Every day." They both agreed.

In dating, it's hard to know if the person you're getting to know will be the best thing that every happened to you or not. But if you find signs that he's not even in the ball park of someone you think could make a major, positive influence on your life, then best to release him. Most long-term happily committed couples would put meeting and/or marrying their mates as one of the best things that ever happened to them, along with the birth of their children.

But some people think sharing something this important would put you in the lower power position, just like the person who utters "I love you" first. Others say "I love you" as cavalierly as "Pass the salt." Both "I love you" and "You are the best thing that ever happened to me" are best saved for after you are in an exclusive, and ideally committed, relationship. Before then you can come off as needy saying either.

Hearing "You are the best thing that ever happened to me" — when backed up by congruent actions, of course — solidify bonds. I believe this can be as significant — or perhaps more so — than hearing "I love you," which has a lot of ambiguity around it these days.

Have you had someone tell you, "You are the best thing that ever happened to me"? If so, how did you feel hearing this?

Permission-based dating over 40

My friend Mike Domitrz is the founder of The Date Safe Project™, and author of *May I Kiss You?* and *Help! My Teen Is Dating*. In familiarizing myself with his work, I was taken not only by his commitment to helping kids and young adults to date more respectfully, but with the application of his ideas to midlife daters.

I've found there are many assumptions in dating over 40. The first kiss is one area. Rarely has a man asked if he could kiss me. Many times a man has kissed me when, if he had asked, I would not have said "yes."

But some people think asking takes all spontaneity and passion out of a kiss. Yet when a man has asked, my respect for him goes up considerably. He is showing me respect, not assuming. Some of the most awkward moments in dating have been when a man I don't want to kiss me does so and I have to quickly extricate myself.

Mike takes it beyond kissing, and says each stage of intimacy should involve permission — no matter who initiates it. By making sure there is explicit permission, it creates more trust, respect and reduces misunderstandings. By asking before moving to the next stage, it gives both parties a chance to pause for a moment and consider what advancing means to them and if they are ready for it.

You may be saying, "This is fine for high school kids. But we are grown adults. We can say no or stop at any time." Yes, we can. But when you are caught up in the moment, you don't always consider, "What will moving the next level really mean? How will my expectations change? Is this something I really want to do, or am I caught up in how good it feels?" I think adults are sometimes only slightly more mature about this than young adults.

Putting the onus on the woman to stop the action is not respectful. I've had men try to talk me out of my "no" which has felt very disrespectful. Wouldn't a man want to have a woman who is fully on board with raising the intimacy, rather than one who is just going with the flow? (I know some men will say, "Either is fine!")

How has your regard changed for a man who asks permission? Have you felt disrespected when a man has just assumed escalating to the next level is fine, putting you in the difficult position of stopping the action?

Midlife crushes

"**C**rush" sounds like a school kid, doesn't it? Remember those feelings of infatuation, exemplified by your hanging out at the crushee's locker or outside the gym as he left practice? Or perhaps you were like me, not-so-subtly keeping score for the team on which the object of your desire played.

In high school, I gave hand-knitted scarves to my unrequited loves. Most were never worn. I baked birthday cakes for my make-believe beaus. Once, the oven rack was tilted, so the cake baked lopsided. Discovering this while removing it from the oven, I crafted a creative fix — raising the lower end with donuts secreted underneath, hidden by frosting. The recipient never mentioned the unusual composition of the cake.

At this point in your life, this seems so, well, childish, right? Crushes are for the emotionally immature, aren't they? Well, no.

Crushes can happen at any age.

The dictionary defines crush as "a brief but intense infatuation for someone, especially someone unattainable or inappropriate." So this feeling is for someone not likely to return your ardor.

For example, a few years ago I developed a crush on my happily married ophthalmologist. He's tall, fit, cute (with a cleft in his chin!), smart, successful (after all, he's a doctor!) and funny. What's not to like? Oh, yeah, there's that part about being married. Ugh. But that didn't keep me from ensuring I always looked my best and giggling at his funny comments when in the exam chair. Or fantasizing about what if he wasn't married.

> *I developed a crush on my happily married ophthalmologist.*

There are low-level crushes and intense crushes. The former is what I have on my auto mechanic's office manager. Do I obsess about this green-eyed, divorced, midlife cutie? No. But I make sure to put on makeup and stylish jeans whenever I take in my car for repair.

An intense crush is when you drive by his house on the weekend hoping to catch him outside or see if his car is in the driveway. Or you just happen to be in his office building when you know he's going to lunch. Or you join his gym even though it's miles out of your way and plant yourself there during his workout times. That's akin to stalking.

The positives of crushes are they rekindle your feelings of aliveness and romantic possibility. The downsides include spending inordinate time and energy focusing on someone who is most likely never going to return your enthusiasm. You are setting yourself up for disappointment if not downright humiliation.

Luckily, my crushees have either ignored my desperately craving their attention, or have graciously accepted my overtures without encouraging me. Perhaps that's part of why they earned my adoration — they embodied kindness.

Have you had midlife crushes? How did you get over obsessing on the unattainable? Or if you've been the object of someone else's crush, how have you discouraged them graciously?

Are you on the same train to boo-ville?

What determines if you are an item? Is it agreement about exclusivity? Is it the fact that neither of you is interested in seeing others?

You may think that his regular calls, texts and weekly dates makes him your beau. He may think that you are just one of the women he is seeing, even if at the moment he's not seeing anyone else. You may feel that by your sleeping together regularly, you are going together. He may feel that you are a woman he's hanging out with.

Don't jump to the conclusion that he feels that you are both on the same train to boo-ville. You may be taking the express and he's taking the local. You are many steps ahead of him, perhaps wanting him to meet your friends and family, taking vacations together, maybe even thinking you'll be moving in together. Yet he's moving at a much slower pace, thinking you are seeing each other and determining if you want to continue. He may not even see you as exclusive unless you've had that discussion.

So don't derail the train by assuming you're on the bullet train to relationship bliss.

Allow yourself to slow down, even if you really like the guy. In fact, throttle back especially if you like the guy as if you make assumptions too fast, he'll jump off the train at the first opportunity. Or throw you off — and ow, that hurts!

Is he a psychopath — or just a manipulator?

At some point in dating you have, no doubt, encountered jerks, players, and self-absorbed individuals. Perhaps you labeled some narcissists. But have you ever encountered someone you'd deem a psychopath?

In researching a relative's extreme personality disorder, I decided to read *Snakes in Suits: When Psychopaths Go to Work* to determine how to best respond to the anti-social behavior with which I was having to deal. While the book focuses on psychopaths in the workplace, I thought I'd glean some ideas for identifying and dealing with these folks anywhere.

First, what's the difference between a narcissist, sociopath and psychopath? I'm not a psychiatrist or psychologist, so I can only paraphrase the authors' description.

"Narcissistic personality disorder involves … displaying a pervasive pattern of grandiosity, need for admiration, sense of entitlement and lack of empathy."

"Sociopathy refers to patterns of attitudes and behaviors that are considered antisocial and criminal by society at large, but are seen as normal ... by the sub-culture ... in which they developed.... Many criminals might be described as sociopaths."

Psychopaths and narcissists have some overlapping characteristics.

Psychopaths and narcissists have some overlapping characteristics, like lack of empathy, and grandiosity, but psychopaths couple these with deceitfulness, lack of remorse, without conscience or loyalty, refusal to accept responsibility and antisocial behavior. While these may sum up the things you loath about your ex, it's not likely he was really a psychopath! More probably, he was probably just a jerk.

Not all psychopaths are criminals — or at least only a fraction of those with this disorder have either committed crimes or have been caught. The authors say approximately 1% of the population could be diagnosed with psychosis. They point out that only a small percentage of them have been put behind bars, so they are loose in society. Because psychopaths are often intelligent and present themselves well, you'd never know to look at them that you are about to be manipulated for your money, job, belongings or sex.

And not all manipulators are psychopaths. There are plenty of people who will lie, cheat, and steal, but that doesn't mean they have this personality disorder.

So if so few people qualify as bona fide psychopaths, why am I telling you all this? Because I found the book a fascinating read and if you deal with anyone — at work or personally — who is a smooth manipulator, it may be useful to you.

Secondly, to encourage you to disengage from anyone who has extremely abnormal behavior that you feel is harmful to you. I had to extricate myself from a bullying manipulator, even amid pleading from friends and family to not do so. I am making that same decision about the aforementioned relative. You don't have to put up with harmful behavior — whether it be emotional, verbal or physical — no matter who it's coming from.

Have you encountered a manipulator in dating? If so, what was the final straw and how did you end it?

Full disclosure

A DG reader shared that he learned his last girlfriend was currently married only after he proposed when she said she was pregnant.

It made me think of what else would be assuring to have someone prove before you got too involved. Of course, it would be considered rude to request the following — at least at the beginning — but it would certainly clarify any questions.

See what you'd add to this list:

💜 Driver's license — I've only found out that one man gave me fictitious personal information, but I've sometimes wondered if a date was who he said he was. Or was the age he claimed, or lived where he stated. A quick look at his driver's license would put at rest any doubts.

💜 Divorce decree — I've had married men tell me they weren't when asked point blank. Honest people say they are separated when not divorced. Dishonest ones say they are divorced or widowed when they aren't. Showing

a divorce decree would prove their status —
unless they'd gotten remarried in the interim.

Credit score/tax returns/net worth statement
— wouldn't it be great if you could exchange
documentation with your suitor to prove each
other's financial soundness? I've been drawn
to people who, after investing months in a
budding relationship, I learned are financially
irresponsible.

Unfortunately, there's not a document one can pro-
duce to show they aren't a convicted felon, a cheater, or
a pathological liar. I've dated the latter two and it took a
while to figure out.

Of course, there is documentation that can show
someone is STD free, but unfortunately few people ask
to see it. If it comes up at all, people just say they are
and the other accepts it. That's just stupid. So even when
documentation is possible, few ask for it.

What documents would you like to see — if there
was actually a way to ask for it without being offensive
— that would prove something about someone before
you got too involved?

Stud finder

When I decided to hang a picture recently, I wished I had a stud finder to ensure the nail went into wood instead of just plaster.

Then it hit me — wouldn't it be great to have a similar tool when looking for a man! One that would guarantee hitting a solid man, not a flaky one. Can you imagine how much easier it would be when you walked into a bar or singles event with one of these devices?

It would light up and sound off when a responsible, solid, upright man was found!

I thought I'd play with this theme when talking to a new man the other night. We'd emailed, texted and talked over the last 2 weeks. But our schedules haven't lined up so we can actually rendezvous. From all indications thus far he seems mature, intelligent, articulate, down-to-earth, responsible, humble and a gentleman.

We were chitchatting, as one does when getting to know one another. I told him of my need to hang a picture and my lack of a stud finder. He told me how great they are; they light up and buzz when a stud is found. I playfully said, "Then I should bring one when we first meet so it will help me locate you."

Without missing a beat, he said, "It will explode."

I nearly fell off my chair laughing. This was so out of character to the humble man I had thought him to be. It wasn't off putting, but instead delightful that he'd come back so quickly with such a funny comment.

So, ladies, let's build our dream Human Stud Finder. I don't mean "stud" in merely the sexual vein, although, of course, that's important. What else would we build into this new tool to help us ferret out the qualities we want? I'll get us going: honesty, caring, romance, intelligence, emotionally stable, financially sound, healthy, responsible.

In addition to other qualities, how do you imagine our invention would work? Should it have an "anti-stud" feature to alert us of those with less-than-quality values? Do we program it with what we're looking for and have it scan the room for those with a high percentage of matches? And assuming men have whatever the equivalent would be, it would be easy to see who is a mutual match.

Now, perhaps we can get someone to program and build this to our specs. We'd make millions!

Getting traction

Midlife singles often tell me that the biggest challenge with dating is getting a date in the first place. That isn't what I see as the greatest obstacle, as you could easily go out with lots of people if you adjust your criteria.

In my experience, the biggest issue is finding someone interesting and engaging enough to see again (and they feel similarly), then building some traction. About half of the 110 men I've gone out with resulted in one-time-only meetings.

By "traction," I mean what the thesaurus gives us: adhesion — or sticking together. While I accept second and subsequent dates with men whose company I enjoy, it can be difficult getting beyond good conversation to a more romantic connection. There is a delicate balance between moving too quickly and moving so slowly that the relationship transitions to the "friend" category.

So how does one get traction toward building a romantic relationship, not just a friendship? I think mutual flirting helps, if sincere, as it telegraphs that you're not just looking for an activity partner pal.

The traction needs to build naturally. If you feel you

are always the one making contact, or suggesting getting together, or pulling the other in conversation, you are in a rut and there is no traction to get you out. You are doing all the heavy lifting in the relationship. That isn't a win/win.

What if you find there is no momentum after a handful of dates? You can continue seeing each other if you like each other, and see if a romantic relationship evolves. I have now-married friends who started out as pals and then they became romantic.

Generally, we expect to feel some spark, some chemistry beyond liking each other. So if you aren't feeling you're becoming more connected, then it's probably best to have the "let's be friends" conversation. That might inspire him to kick it up a notch and realize he wants more, or he might just agree to be friends.

What have you done if you don't feel the relationship is moving forward after a handful of dates? Have you stuck with it or relegated the relationship into the friend realm?

Authenticity vs. strategic phoniness

I was listening to my friend Mike Robbins speak to a group about his newest book on authenticity, *Be Yourself. Everyone Else is Already Taken: Transform Your Life with the Power of Authenticity.* He'd asked the audience a few questions about what value authenticity has in our lives and then he asked why being authentic was so hard.

Several people shared that being authentic meant being vulnerable which wasn't always optimal, especially in business. There was much agreement that one should be their authentic self, no matter what. Phoniness was not compelling.

I raised my hand and said, "I struggle with strategic phoniness. For example, if I'd shown up for this event without makeup or Spanx, you wouldn't have wanted to be around me. My authentic self wears neither, but it doesn't represent the me I want you to know. So when is strategic phoniness acceptable?"

A lively discussion ensued about how looking one's

best wasn't really phony.

> *We want to put our best selves forward.*

It made me think about dating. We want to put our best selves forward, but where is the line between presenting ourselves in the best possible light and being inauthentic? We think certain elements of our personality are unattractive so we should keep those hidden until we know someone better and feel they won't reject us for those.

However, a common complaint in dating is that someone didn't turn out as they represented themselves. He appeared successful, wearing expensive clothes or spending lavishly on dates. Only when you were hooked emotionally to him, did you learn he was deep in debt.

Or he snuggled up next to you during your favorite TV shows or sports, seemingly engaged, but once you are committed (or married!) he shows no interest whatsoever. The new wife of my cousin confided that when they were dating, they would work out together 5 times a week. Now that they are married, she can't get him to the gym.

Or when dating, they'd have sex regularly. Both

seemed to really enjoy it. Now that they are living together, you can count on one hand the number of intimate times they share each month.

So where's the line between wanting to seem like a
good sport and participate in your sweetie's activities,
and when you're being inauthentic? You fear that if you
are truly authentic ("No, I don't want to hang out with
your bratty grandkids this weekend"), you won't find
anyone to date. However, when is "going along" and
"being a good sport" turn into pretending something
that isn't true for you?

What's your take on the distinction between authenticity and strategic phoniness? Have you been disappointed when someone you thought was authentic
turned out to be different?

I want to date his family

It's a bit awkward when someone you're newly getting to know invites you to a casual family event and you end up hitting it off with his family much more than you do with him!

> *You end up hitting it off with his family much more than you do with him!*

This happened to me this weekend. My new activity partner (AP) and I had agreed to see a movie. He called at noon to see if I'd like to have a bite to eat beforehand. "Sure" I responded. Then he added, "We'll go to my brother's for a BBQ, then we can go to the movie."

"Hmmm" I thought. "We're only activity partners, not really dating, and we've only seen each other 3 times before. It's kinda early to be meeting his family. But what the heck, maybe it's a party and I'm his plus one."

It was not a party. It was just the four of us.

I hit it off immediately with his brother and sister-in-law. Especially the brother. He was tall, good looking, smart, funny and closer to my age and temperament than my activity partner. But he was married. How I wished he wasn't — I'd be flirting up a storm.

His sister-in-law was sweet. But the contrast between the two of them and my AP was jarring. He is a sweet man, but he repeats himself and only talks about what he did on his job — from which he retired 8 years ago.

By the end of the afternoon, I restrained myself from suggesting we all go to a movie together. Asking for a second "date" seemed presumptive. So we'll see if my AP comes up with this on his own.

Have you experienced liking your date's friends or family better than him?

To play games or not?

Deb writes:

> *"I have had 4 dates with one man and I find him very interesting, funny, smart and a gentleman. How do I tell if he is really interested in me? I have read books and everything says to play a game, acting like you are not interested and he will come after you. I want an honest, open and upfront relationship. Do I tell him that I like him and flat out ask if he feels the same. Or do I go with the game of acting like I am not interested?"*

Ah, Deb. The age-old question of, "Do I turn him off if I show I'm interested, or pretend to be aloof and coy in the hopes of enticing him?"

This conundrum has plagued women for decades (nay, centuries?).

First, I'm never for playing games. I, like you, prefer to be straightforward. That said, timing and word choice are everything. If you ask "Are you interested in me long term?" in the first few dates, you'll sound needy and inappropriate.

I think the key is not what is *said* but what is done. Even if he answered, "Yes, I'm interested in you long term" then did little to show his interest, his actions (or inactions) create confusion and frustration, but really show his interest level. So it's almost a moot point what you ask or what he says. You look for the actions that show he cares.

Caveat: In "Signs of endearment — or just habits?" I discuss how I misinterpreted what I thought were signs of caring, when really they were just my then-beaus habits around any woman. So actions nor words on their own are beacons into his thoughts and heart.

So my advice is to continue to show interest in him, accept his invitations, smile and laugh, but go slow. Look for the signs that says he's interested in you beyond a quick fling. His introducing you to his friends and family is a solid sign, but it's not the only thing to look for.

In other words, don't broach the "Do you like me?" conversation. Keep it light and fun. When he brings it up, it will be more likely he wants to get more serious.

Resources

Make sure to download your free eBook Attract Your Next Great Mate: Dating Advice From Top Relationship Experts at www.Dating-Goddess.com/freebie

Afterword

At the time of this writing, I have not yet found my true King Charming. I continue my search with verve. I've become more discerning about what I want and don't want. I've met some wonderful men pals — my treasures — who continue to be in touch.

I wish you much luck in your adventure. It will be fun and frustrating, exhilarating and exasperating, and sexy or sexless. So much depends on you, your approach and your attitude. My books are designed to help you enjoy as much as possible and ward off unpleasantness. But nearly all adventures have wonderful highs as well as a few lows. If you know that going in and arm yourself with information on what to expect, you'll have more of the positives and fewer of the negatives.

Please drop by www.DatingGoddess.com and join in the discussion and report on your experiences.

Dating Goddess

$\mathcal{R}$esources

Go to www.datinggoddess.com to access a variety of useful resources. We work to suggest resources we think have value.

Dating and relationship book reviews

These reviews will save you time and money as I've given you my take on specific books, CDs and more. Some are worth your effort to buy and read or listen to them — some are not. We're always adding new book reviews, so check frequently. We'll also notify our mailing list when new resources are added.

Dating site links

There are a lot of dating sites on the Internet. I've listed the ones I think are worth investigating.

Dating products and tools

Dating can be daunting. We're continually looking at

ways to make it easier and more fun. We'll provide info on games, tools, even date-wear that will help others know you're available, or help you get to know potential suitors better.

Dating and relationship advice sites

Advice "experts" abound on the Internet as anyone can self-proclaim themseves as expert — even if they haven't dated in 30 years and never in midlife. I've worked to find experts who's advice I generally think is solid.

Midlife recources

We'll feature Web sites, books, events and other resources we think might interest you.

Newly discovered resources

I'll add other resources as we discover them, subscribe to our mailing list to get the scoop as soon as we find them. Go to www.DatingGoddess.com to register for our mailing list. Don't worry, we won't sell or give your email to anyone.

Acknowledgments

Let me start by acknowledging the 112 men who helped trigger the lessons contained in this book. Some prompted several! They remain nameless here to protect their identity, although most would recognize references to them. Plus the thousands more whose winks, emails and calls didn't result in a date, but helped me learn the dating game. And all those men who I emailed who never responded — such a blessing to have them weed themselves out.

I acknowledge the 112 men who triggered my lessons

I'd like to thank my Seven Sisters mastermind group for the tremendous brainstorming, noodling, strategizing and encouragement. I wouldn't have begun this project without the prodding of Val Cade, Chris Clarke-Epstein, Mariah Burton Nelson, Sue Dyer, Sam Horn and Marilynn Mobley.

Thank you to my good friends who've listened to my dating stories ad nauseam, and whose support and wisdom are embedded in this text. Ed Betts, Ken Braly, Bruce Daley, Tom Drews, Elaine Floyd, Paulette Ensign, Scott Friedman, Craig Harrison, Mary Jansen, Tom Johnson, Sandy Jones, Mary Kilkenny, Ellie Klevins, Patrick Lynch, Mary Marcdante, Barbara McNichol, Ann Peterson, Anthony Ramsey, Caterina Rando, Kristy Rogers, Jana Stanfield, Holly Steil, Terry Tepliz, and George Walther, thank you.

The Adventures in Delicious Dating After 40 series

The Adventures in Delicious Dating After 40 series is designed to help you understand your own midlife dating journey. It is not a road map, as we all take different routes. It is a guide to help you understand yourself, midlife men, and the dating process. Hopefully, you'll not only learn from the lessons and insights shared in this series, but you'll examine how they apply — or don't — to your own dating adventure.

You'll get the scoop on what you need to know, what's changed since you last dated, and how to navigate inevitable bumps in the road.

Following is an overview of each book in the series and a sampling of some of the chapter titles. All are detailed at www.DatingGoddess.com.

Date or Wait: Are You Ready for Mr. Great?

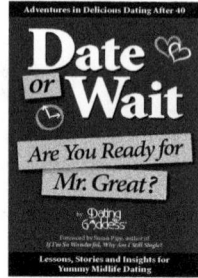

Are you ready for a special man in your life? You have a great life. But you know you'd like a special man to share it. You think you're ready to date, but you haven't done it in a while.

What should you consider before you actually start dating full bore? Even if you've reentered the dating world, this will give you a foundation of attitude and philosophy to make your adventure more fulfilling.

Sample chapters

💚 From hurt to flirt

💚 Dating is like Baskin-Robbins

💚 You've got to kiss a lot of…princes!

💚 What's your definition of dating success?

💚 Are you open to receiving?

💚 Dating: A self-designed personal-growth workshop

💚 Hands-on dating research

💚 Being present to the presents

💚 Being aggressively single

💚 Approaching dating like a buffet

💚 Is Brad Pitt ruining your love life?

💚 Treasures can come in dented packages

Assessing Your Assets: Why You're A Great Catch

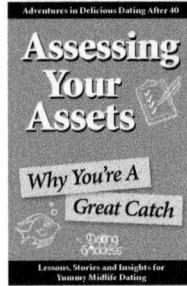

You have many wonderful qualities. But it's easy to focus on one's flaws — at least what seem like flaws to you. However, to the right man your imperfections are endearing, attractive and lovable. You have to be clear what you offer a man who will find you enchanting.

Assessing Your Assets helps you look at what you bring to a new relationship. It will help you see your good points so you'll approach dating with more confidence.

Sample chapters

❤ Don't think you are damaged goods

❤ You are (probably) more attractive than you think!

❤ They aren't called "hate handles"

❤ Are you a good man picker?

❤ What are your deal breakers?

❤ Are you arguing your limitations?

❤ Turn your liabilities into assets

❤ The strong vs. nice woman debate

❤ Is your sense of humor stunting your dating?

❤ Why are we drawn to bad boys?

❤ The zest test

In Search of King Charming: Who Do I Want to Share My Throne?

You are no longer looking for "Prince" Charming because you are a queen. You want someone who is at your level, not groveling at your feet. You want a king — someone who's your equal and with whom you can rule the throne together!

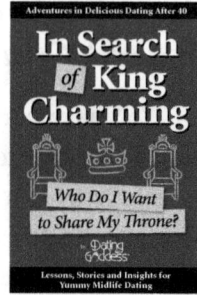

This book focuses on helping you better define what you want beyond tall, dark and handsome! You'll consider characteristics you might not have thought of before. You'll look at what you want now.

Sample chapters

💚 Building your Franken-boyfriend

💚 What's your "perfect boyfriend's" job description?

💚 A man to go with your wardrobe

💚 In search of the elusive good kisser

💚 When you're clear on what you want, it appears

💚 Are you dating the same guy in different bodies?

💚 Does he fit in your world?

💚 What's your kissing quotient?

💚 Is your guy's loving muscle strong?

💚 Do you both have the same dating rhythm?

Embracing Midlife Men: Insights Into Curious Behaviors

Do you sometimes scratch your head after interacting with a midlife man, wondering, "What could he possibly be thinking?" Especially if it's before, during or after a date with a man who presumably wants to impress you!

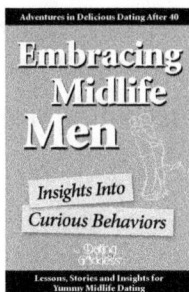

This book focuses on better understanding midlife men's behaviors. When you grasp what's going on in his head it's much easier to embrace him. Men are wondrous creatures, so we need to understand them better and love them for who they are.

Sample chapters

💜 Men are like shoes

💜 Why men disappear when it gets serious

💜 Chivalry isn't dead —but it seems to be hibernating

💜 Do men want feisty women?

💜 Midlife men have forgotten how to date

💜 Are you getting prime time from your man?

💜 When a man tells you what he paid for things

💜 Does he treat you like his ex?

💜 Has Greg Behrendt done women a disservic

💜 Tales of woo

Dipping Your Toe in the Dating Pool: Dive In Without Belly Flopping

You've decided you are ready — you want to start dating. Maybe you've already had a few coffee dates with several men. You want to be as successful as possible on your dating adventure.

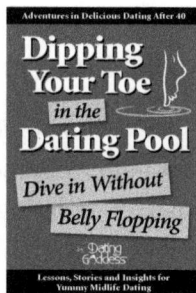

This book focuses on getting started on your dating adventures. We cover what you need to know as you begin your journey.

Sample chapters

💚 Do you have the right datewear?

💚 Dating with integrity

💚 Building your rejection muscle

💚 When "be yourself" is questionable advice

💚 Faux beaus and practice dating

💚 Are you making bad decisions out of loneliness?

💚 Being "in wonder" about your date's behavior

💚 When do you feel most vulnerable in dating?

💚 Are you out of his league — or he yours?

💚 Why listening is so seductive

Winning at the Online Dating Game: Stack the Deck in Your Favor

Internet dating can be frustrating or fruitful. It will be much less exasperating if you know how to read and weed out men's profiles that aren't appropriate for you. And you'll have a steady stream of potential suitors if you know how to write a compelling profile for yourself.

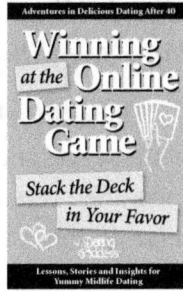

This book focuses on the ins and outs of online dating. How to play the game, which has it's own rules and language. If you don't understand how online dating works, you'll waste a lot of time connecting with men who are not a possible fit for you.

Sample chapters

💜 Shopping for men

💜 Safe online dating

💜 Is 21st Century dating unnatural?

💜 What do men look at in your profile?

💜 Euphemisms uncovered

💜 Are you describing yourself compellingly?

💜 No, I will not be dating your Harley

💜 Playing the online dating game

💜 Scantily clothed pictures

Check Him Out Before Going Out: Avoiding Dud Dates

Under the cloak of the anonymity that email and the phone provides, men often reveal more than they intend. If you ask the right questions you can find out a lot about his values and view of the world after just an interaction or two.

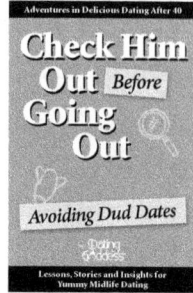

This book focuses on what you need to ask before agreeing to even a coffee date. You need to vet the men who email and call you to ensure you're not likely to waste your time with men who clearly aren't a match.

Sample chapters

💜 Becoming smitten with the fantasy

💜 Can Google help — or hinder — your dating life?

💜 Qualify your potential dates before meeting

💜 The art of consideration

💜 Anticipating a big date is like awaiting Santa

💜 Being seduced by what he is over who he is

💜 Are you his spare?

💜 My boyfriend, whom I haven't met

💜 When canceling is the right thing to do

💜 Politics, religion and sex — oh my!

First-Rate First Dates: Increasing the Chances of a Second Date

You can tell a lot about someone within the first 30 minutes. What does he talk about? Does he ask you questions? If so, what does he want to know about you? What do you need to know about him? How does he treat you? How does he treat those around you?

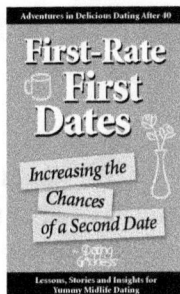

Adventures in Delicious Dating After 40

First-Rate First Dates

Increasing the Chances of a Second Date

Lessons, Stories and Insights for Yummy Midlife Dating

This book focuses on what goes on during the first date. How do you determine if you want a second date? What you can do to increase the likelihood your date will ask you for a second? That is if you want a repeat!

Sample chapters

💚 Start with coffee

💚 How do you greet him?

💚 When it clicks, throw out some of your criteria

💚 Tracking your date's score

💚 Clues a guy is just looking for a booty call

💚 12 signs he won't be asking for a second date

💚 First-date red flags that this guy isn't for you

💚 Honesty is not always the best policy

💚 Chemistry, or does he make my toes curl?

💚 Women's first-date blunders

Real Deal or Faux Beau: Should You Keep Seeing Him?

You've begun to go out with a man you like. How do you decide if you should continue seeing him, or if you should release him because he's not The One?

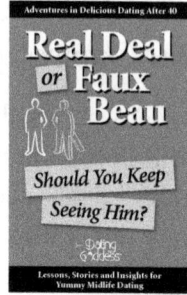

This book focuses on second dates and beyond. During the dating process you are both assessing if you want to keep seeing each other. This book helps you determine what questions you need to ask yourself.

Sample chapters

💜 Deciding to see him again or not

💜 What's your date's Delight/Disappointment Scale score?

💜 Broaching tough conversations

💜 "I want to respect me in the morning"

💜 Does he invite you to his place?

💜 Are you stingy in dating?

💜 When his hand is on your knee too soon

💜 Easy way to ask hard questions

💜 Rose-colored glasses obscure red flags

💜 If his stories don't add up, subtract yourself

Multidating Responsibly: Play the Field Without Being A Player

Playing the field is frowned on in some circles. There are definitely appropriate and inappropriate ways to date several men simultaneously.

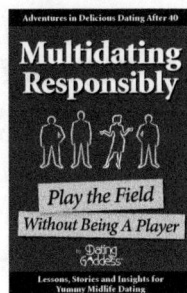

This book focuses on how to date around responsibly and with integrity without leading men on. If you do it with honesty, you can date several people at once until you're both ready to focus only on each other.

Sample chapters

💜 "Pimpin'" — Dating multiple guys

💜 Multi-dating pros and cons

💜 Your Date-A-Base — tracking multiple suitors

💜 "Hot bunking" your beaus

💜 Are you a "Let's Make a Deal" type of dater?

💜 Assume there are other women

💜 Dating's revolving door

💜 How long do you hedge your bet?

💜 Beware of multi-tasking when multi-dating

💜 Back burner beaus

💜 The boyfriend phone

Moving On Gracefully: Break Up Without Heartache

"Breaking up" sounds so high school, doesn't it? But part of the dating process is saying something when one of you decides not to date the other anymore. Going "poof" is not a mature or respectful option in midlife.

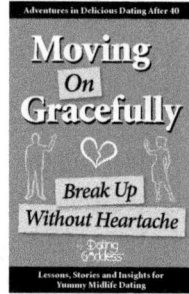

This book focuses on surviving a breakup, whether you initiate it or not. Either way, it's never easy to break up if you have developed any fondness toward the other.

Sample chapters

💚 Hello — goodbye: How to say no thanks after meeting

💚 Releasing back into the dating pool

💚 50 ways to leave your lover? 4 ways not to leave your suitor

💚 Breaking up is hard to do — right

💚 Why men go "poof"

💚 How to trump being dumped

💚 When breaking up is a "Get Out of Jail Free" card

💚 How to detect the end is near

💚 Failed relationships' blessings

💚 He's broken up with you — he just didn't tell you

💚 Rejection is protection

From Fear to Frolic: Get Naked Without Getting Embarrassed

This book focuses on what you need to consider and know before getting physically intimate with a man you're dating. This is nerve-wracking to many midlife women. This book will prepare you.

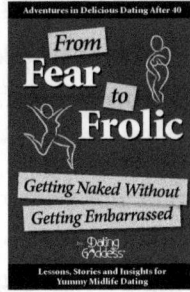

Sample chapters

- Sleepover do's and don'ts
- Does he want in your life — or just in your bedroom?
- Getting naked with him the first time
- An excuse to seduce or how important is bedroom bliss?
- What to ask yourself before getting naked with him
- Are you and your guy on the same sexual time line?
- Sharing your sexual owner's manual with him
- What women need from a man before having sex
- Why too-soon midlife sex is like non-fat food
- How dating sex is like waffles
- Too-soon seduction: "I'm special, but not THAT special"

Ironing Out Dating Wrinkles: Work Through Challenges Without Getting Steamed

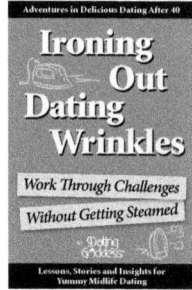

Nearly all relationships have some ups and downs. Part of getting to know someone is knowing how they work through relationship misunderstandings.

This book focuses on how to work through the inevitable hiccups that happen when you are getting to know each other. If you can both deal with challenges, the bond deepens and you find yourself smitten.

Sample chapters

- When your guy vexes you, ask what your highest self would do
- The first fight
- You want boo; he wants boo-ty
- Where's the line between getting your needs met and being selfish?
- Expressing your upset with your guy
- Is his toothbrush in your cabinet too soon?
- Do you love how he loves you?
- Is he collecting data on how to make you happy?
- Be careful of being smitten
- Exclusivity: How and when to broach it